EARLY
AMERICAN HOMES
FOR TODAY

GOVERNOR GALUSHA HOUSE, SHAFTSBURY
Part of east front

HERBERT WHEATON CONGDON

EARLY AMERICAN HOMES FOR TODAY

A Treasury of Decorative Details and Restoration Procedures

CHARLES E. TUTTLE COMPANY
RUTLAND, VERMONT

European Representatives

For the Continent:
BOXERBOOKS, INC., Zurich

For the British Isles:
PRENTICE-HALL INTERNATIONAL INC., London

Published by the Charles E. Tuttle Company
of Rutland, Vermont & Tokyo, Japan
with editorial offices at
15 Edogawa-cho, Bunkyo-ku, Tokyo

Library of Congress Catalog
Card No. 62–18936

First printing, 1963

Book design and typography by Kaoru Ogimi
PRINTED IN JAPAN

CONTENTS

LIST OF ILLUSTRATIONS*

* *All examples illustrated are from the State of Vermont and are here arranged by county and town.*

EARLY
AMERICAN HOMES
FOR TODAY

OLD TAVERN, MARLBORO
View from northwest

[I]

OUR HERITAGE

——◆·●·◆——

THIS BOOK is intended to be a help to the do-it-yourself man who has had the good fortune to come into the possession of one of New England's old homes. It describes and illustrates a considerable variety of old-time designs of several periods, which might be used on its exterior or indoors. It should help the man who is "handy with tools," or any intelligent carpenter of the neighborhood, to make the most of a neglected but worthy old building. It could also be a safe guide in building a new house in the old style, which might be more vital than the usual undistinguished "Colonial" too often seen in Suburbia. Materials may be bought at the local mill and mouldings altered in the home workshop.

The most important preparation for such a project is to get the *feeling* of the best of the old work, to study the buildings themselves, if possible, as well as their details. As an aid to this, the illustrations in this book are not only general views of the whole but in many cases are accompanied by large-scale detail pictures. In addition, in the front of the book there is a list of all the illustrations which is arranged geographically—a suggestive guide to the back-road explorer. No photograph can take the place of a thoughtful perception of the real thing.

A couple who had strong feelings about that sort of study were following a little-used road, "passable but rough" in local parlance. It led through an old countryside, a neighborhood with many abandoned farms, almost breath-taking in beauty. They hoped to find a summer home and realized that land classed as submarginal by farmers might be fertile in the qualities for which they sought— a refuge from city crowds. They stopped to eat their sandwiches where they could look out for miles between the trunks of a row of sturdy old maples protected by a mossy stone wall. The neglected meadow, green with tall, fragrant June grass, sloped gently down to a brush-lined brook. Beyond, it rose again to far, forested hills. A bobolink sang in mid-air, then dove to his nest. Above, the sky was incredibly blue. Farther along the road they could see the gable of a house, sleeping in the sunshine, waiting for those who wanted its shelter. When they got back in the car the man said, "I wonder if that is the old Robinson place they told us about, back in the village? They said he chose it for the view, after he had camped for the night on his long tramp back from the war to his family home. Could be. Let's look."

When they got to the house they walked all around it, even went inside through the decrepit cellarway. The house was in rather bad condition. The man's fingers itched for the tools that were back home and his wife dreamed of restoring the old stencil work on a plastered wall, now half fallen.

"Remember? We had lots of fun playing house when we were kids. That one we fixed up in your back yard. I've an idea we could do it again, this time with a *real* house, recapture that excitement and happiness by fixing up this one. Notice how *friendly* it feels, as if it liked us? We played at being Father and Mother then, when we were just neighbors. Now it's true. How about playing the game again?" This is a true story. They bought the place, and working with local help they restored it, making the few changes needed by modern ways of living so skilfully that it seems obvious that they and their helpers thought in the same way as their ancestors.

The essential thing for the do-it-yourself man is that he embellishes or restores an old house *appropriately*, avoiding discord in style. Good taste accepts major additions in a later development of the Colonial style to an older house of the same period, but to add a wing in "Ranch House" to a Colonial main building would obviously be an error. The additions to Ebenezer Robinson's simple little home that are shown in later pages are harmonious; the restorations made a hundred years later recognize this. And what fun the owners had while doing the work !

The chapters that follow deal with exterior and interior features. They show illustrations of a wide variety of characteristic details used in different periods, by which an owner may be guided, whether in his own home craftsman's work or in directing one of the many local workmen who have absorbed the "feeling"

1: PARSON DEWEY HOUSE, OLD BENNINGTON
A gabled house with central chimney

of our old houses by living in and with them. His project may include additions to the plan of the building or even building anew in the old style. It may be only adding desirable decorative features to an overly plain room, or giving a needed focus to the house-front by a better entrance. It may entail demolishing a jig-sawed Victorian piazza that hides a fine doorway or replacing a fireplace and its mantel removed back in the 1840's when stoves were first used to add to the comfort of the family. All of these problems have been faced. They can be solved successfully only if the design is appropriate to the house.

Vermont's oldest dwellings were very plain, partly from the lack of money, partly from a preference for simplicity. One of the oldest homes that has been occupied continuously is in Old Bennington (Fig. 1). It was built in 1763 for, and largely by, the Rev. Jedediah Dewey, the first pastor of the Congregational Church in that quiet hilltop village. Its perfect proportions, the shapes and placings of its doors and windows, and even the location and bulk of its single chimney combine to give it a serene charm, a sense of belonging there. It stands today, practically unchanged and in excellent physical condition. This is not a building that needs any ornamental details of cornice or trim.

Vermont was not settled until the latter part of the 1700's. The pioneers were hard-working, thrifty men, usually with large families brought up in that tradition. They were "handy with tools" as a matter of necessity and freely helped one another when help was needed, as in building a home. Those virtues resulted, naturally, in a general increase of prosperity. With the passage of time, those who had special skills could be hired, and in that manner the "housewright" was developed. The first, ultra-plain houses of the pioneers were not only too small for the bigger families, but their owners had memories of the handsome dwellings of their earlier lives, and the desire grew for homes that were not only larger, but handsomer than their first ones. These were built on the typical plan of what we now call a Colonial house. Newcomers to the neighborhood, skilled in house building, brought in the previously unknown moulding planes and similar tools of their trade that they had won when they graduated from their apprenticeships elsewhere in New England. With these they could make handsome details.

Often these houses were built so they connected with the old one, which became a wing or ell of the new home and was apt to be made over, inside and out, to match the new work. Sometimes a modern owner gets a surprise when making repairs in the wing, finding that it was originally a log cabin which had been concealed by skins of inside plastering and outside clapboards.

Vermont's Colonial style has persisted through successive waves of fashion, Greek Revival, Victorian Gothic, and today's Ranch House design. Evidently, people like it. It is hard to say whether this persistence is due entirely to the housewrights. They followed the wishes of their clients then, as now. However, they developed artistically even if few of them had access to books on architecture. Some of them may have been apprenticed to and studied design under masters in the older states.

These master builders or, as we would call them today, architects, worked with their hands as well as their heads, with the other workmen on the job. In addition, our early architects were also contractors, a combination now forbidden to the profession by the American Institute of Architects. We know the

2: HINSDILL HOUSE, BENNINGTON
Note the entrance bay

names of very few of them. Of these, Lavius Fillmore of Bennington and Middlebury is known for the designs of the notable meeting houses in those villages. A number of handsome residences, especially in the vicinity of Bennington, are also his work. Thoroughly trained, it is evident, in the classical ways, he was Vermonter enough to use his ingenuity and excellent taste in changing conventional details.

The Hinsdill (Hinsdale?) House, with its unconventional Palladian window, is one of these (Fig. 2). It suggests that he owned some of the English books of the period, for it is an excellent translation into wood of a stone-trimmed brick house of the Georgian period in England. The skill with which he has adapted it to Yankee materials and an unpretentious Vermont setting is admirable. So is the way he has designed the entrance door and the window above it, forming what architects term an "entrance bay." It is a touch of genius, and has suggestions for a modern owner whose house is overly plain, for this focus of the com-

3: HARRIS HOUSE, CASTLETON
With Victorian piazza

4: HARRIS HOUSE, CASTLETON
Piazza removed

5: SOULE HOUSE, FAIRFIELD
Old stairs, Victorian newel

position changes the building from "nicely proportioned but uninteresting" to a really distinguished one. While this example may be too ambitious for the average home craftsman to copy, Chapter IV has simpler ones among its illustrations, and a good deal may be seen in other illustrations that may be useful.

The Colonial architecture of Vermont, like that of its neighboring states, is marked by simplicity and serenity. The Victorian style is the exact opposite, characterized by fussiness, meaningless jigsawed ornament, and a very low level of taste. Houses built in that style a hundred years or more ago are difficult to make over, due in part to strange towers and similar excrescences in the plan, and to poorly proportioned door and window openings. Fortunately for owners of today, older dwellings that were originally built in the earlier style but have been overlaid with Victorian additions can be restored. It was during the prosperous days just before and after the Civil War that honest and really old houses were "improved" by building piazzas across their fronts. These may have been welcome shelters for those who sat in their shade on summer days, watching the lazy horse-drawn traffic drift by, but today there is less leisure and the noisy, and often malodorous, automobile traffic leaves them unused and unlovely masks to what was once a beautiful building.

Demolition is the answer and may work miracles. Figures 3 and 4, "before and after" pictures of the same house-front, tell the story better than could be done by many words. It is almost a major operation in house-surgery, but can be done by unskilled labor and at very small cost. It is obvious from these detail pictures that the piazza was so insistent in attracting the eye that the fine entrance door and Palladian window above it were not noticed. Even the beautiful eaves treatment, while not concealed, was seldom perceived. By great good luck those who had erected this piazza did not do any damage to the upper part of the doorway, they just boxed it in. The cost of demolition and repair to the clapboards was trivial in comparison to the increase in charm of the house, which is shown again in the body of Chapter II (Fig. 10). Of course, in some cases the removal of a similar concealment may reveal a very plain and uninteresting front door. This may easily be bettered by even a tyro in house carpentry, if he uses one of the door treatments shown by the pictures in Chapter IV.

Similarly, Victorian errors indoors may be corrected to the advantage of the householder. A very unusual stairway in a large and beautiful home in the northern part of the state had its newel post replaced by a Victorian black-walnut monstrosity (Fig. 5), which may have been inspired by a piano leg. What the original newel may have looked like we do not know, but there are suggestions to be found in Chapter V. The treatment of the string (the face of the stairway) with an ivy vine, is unique. Think of the labor of carving this. The big timber, notched to receive the steps, had its surface cut away for its entire length, leaving the vine in relief! This same motif appears outdoors, running the entire length of the frieze of the eaves treatment. Even in those days, the cost must have been staggering. Why ivy, instead of the conventional, Classic ornament in the frieze of an entablature which could have been of carpenter-made pieces of wood nailed on? Nobody knows.

Elaboration from the utter plainness of the Parson Dewey House is within the capability of a home craftsman. It is not necessary to go to the extremes shown in Chapters III and IV, beautiful as these may be, and in the interior of the house especially, very satisfying results may be had by simple embellishments shown and discussed in Chapters VI and IX. Much depends, of course, on the condition of the house that is to be restored or improved, the amount of decoration and whether it be indoors or out. For that reason it seems reasonable to classify the old houses, to form three groups.

Group One consists of dwellings that have been kept in good repair through all their long life and essentially unaltered during that time. They are profitable examples for study and, while few in number, they may be found in widely scattered parts of the state. Some of them are still owned by the families of their original builders and naturally are cherished. It is seldom that a house in this group may be bought, but their owners are usually sympathetic to the interest displayed by serious students.

Group Two includes houses that may be in excellent condition but have suffered from unwise "improvements" during waves of architectural fashions, especially in the Victorian era. Some of these changes have been so extensive that from the outside, the building appears to be merely a commonplace product of the late nineteenth century. In this group also, are houses that look as if they belonged in Group One, but have been completely modernized inside during the Black Walnut period. Occasionally, fine old mantels may be stored in the barn, either replaced by tasteless white marble ones, or surplus, because fireplaces and even chimneys have been removed or rebuilt. The house shown in Figure 2 belongs to this highly miscellaneous group, most of the lovely old trim having been replaced by black walnut, lacking charm of design.

There is always the chance, however, that some excellent old features have not been removed, but concealed or plastered over in the course of "improvements," like the china cabinet shown in Figure 81, or the stencil work on the walls, Figure 85. Of course a new owner always hopes to find forgotten or hidden treasures in an old house he has bought. Few have the luck of the man who bought a very plain building which had housed one family for many generations. The last of this line, a recluse, died there, leaving the neglected roof leaks unrepaired. The new owner, stripping away falling plaster and old, rotted lath, found, beneath the dirt and wreckage, that two of the rooms were completely paneled, the handsomest in the state!

Group Three is also a mixed one, for the houses in it may cover the entire age range. These are dwellings that *never* had any ornamental details, inside or out, yet are well proportioned with door and window openings harmonious to one another and to the whole façade, and the physical condition as good as when they were built. They are barren of charm. They are not "has-beens," but truly "never-was-its." To beautify a building of this group is a challenge to the new owner, almost a civic duty. Provided with suitable ornamental details inside and out it can be made to blossom into a noteworthy home. Only the neighbors need recognize the alteration, if it is appropriately and skilfully done. Besides increasing its resale value far beyond the cost of the work, what a good time a man could have, doing this creative work. Being his own master, he can do it a little at a time. It might be that a new front-door trim is all that is needed now. That trim may be developed later into such an entrance as may be found in Chapter IV.

Many old houses in this group do not date back to the days of hewn frames (discussed in the next chapter) but nevertherless are well built. The floor framing may be seen by looking up from the cellar, and this will also show whether there was originally a chimney with fireplaces. If so, there are many suggestions for mantels in Chapter IX and there is much information about constructing efficient and safe chimneys and fireplaces in Chapters VII and VIII.

Restoring an old house or merely embellishing one has its risks. The maligned Victorians honestly thought they were improving on the Colonial style. They knew little, and apparently cared less, about our heritage. We, with what we believe to be wider knowledge and better taste, may well be a little cautious before we start any project. We may smile at the story of the old man, known for uncanny skill in finding strayed cattle, who explained that all he did was to sit down and "try to think like a heifer. Then I go right to wh'ar she ought to be, and thar she is." With that attitude of mind, a previously inexperienced man can approach his problem if he tries to understand the *minds* of the builders—and their clients—who worked almost a century and a half ago. This book provides general and detailed pictures of their work. It shows doors and windows, staircases and mantels, and a wealth of mouldings and other ornamental details that they used. From these examples we may be able to adapt modern materials to obtain similar, or at least harmonious, effects.

We know what they did, we can guess how they did it. It is less easy to grasp *why* they did things that way. Occasionally we may notice some of their errors in judgment. Take, for example, Jonas Galusha of Shaftsbury. We can think of him as one of the "common ancestors" of the home craftsmen of today. He lived in pioneer days when it was taken as a matter of course that a farmer could do anything, some things better than others, perhaps. That was only to be expected. He was the youngest of five sons, and at eighteen years of age was described as "short and sturdy, rosy of complexion, blue-eyed and full of fun." In addition, we know he had somewhere learned how to make the hand-wrought iron nails that were used in those days and that in his youth he had developed a lucrative little business in the times when he could be spared from working on his father's farm. He liked people and as long as he lived kept on making friends. He made money, too, but never changed from the simple, modest man who was an efficient Captain of Militia in the Revolutionary War and served his state as governor for *nine* one-year terms besides being a successful farmer and innkeeper.

He was one of those whose house grew too small for his family, so he called on Lavius Fillmore to design one that would supply his needs. Fillmore was a busy man, glad to turn over the "draught" to Galusha, from which he and his sons built the house still standing, in perfect condition, alongside the highway from Bennington to Burlington. If one looks at its details it is plain that the Galushas did pretty much as they pleased about them. The stairway, for example, is about what might have been expected (Fig. 68), but the step-ends are crudely shaped and of much thicker wood than is generally used for that sort of ornament. The contrast with the finer craftsmanship of the mantels is marked. Those may have been made by Fillmore's men, for the one in the "best bedchamber" is distinguished and of very unusual design. It is illustrated in Chapter IX.

There is a legend connected with that room. A foreigner came to the inn late one afternoon, pack on back, asking for room and board. He was one of that little-known band of men who roamed New England in the days before wallpaper came into use, decorating the walls of those who wanted something better than bare plaster, but who could not afford the costly imported scenic wallpaper. They did their work with special paints, applied through stencils which they combined in ways to make a wide variety of designs as well as of colors. This man seemed to have great difficulty in finding customers. Perhaps his long

6: GOVERNOR GALUSHA HOUSE, SHAFTSBURY
Doorway and part of wall, best bedroom

daily tramps made him unduly thirsty. At any rate, the score chalked on the
back of the barroom door grew so big that even kindly Jonas lost his temper and
set the man to work, decorating the walls of the best bedchamber in order to
settle his bill before he took to the road.

He did a good job as far as permanence was concerned, for it is there today,
a silent witness to the tale. Most amazingly, he did not seem to have any stencils,
the chief stock in trade of his craft. All the work was done freehand and in very
few colors. It suggests that he placed great faith in John Barleycorn as his helper,
for the patterns vary oddly in size where they are repeated, and linear rectitude
"is purely coincidental" (Fig. 6).

One of the governor's older brothers, Jacob, built a larger house on the other
side of the highway and about half a mile distant. The comparison of the two
dwellings is interesting, for Jacob, older and it may be wealthier, seems to have
employed the same architect. His house was evidently built by skilled labor
where Jonas and his sons did much of the erection of their home with little help
of that sort. Jacob's entrance porch, for example, is of the same design as the
governor's. It has finer details, its columns are more slender. Jonas and his sons
liked the thicker ones which the Frontispiece shows and may have rigged up
their own lathe in which to turn them. The mantels and other interior trim in
Jacob's house are more delicate and sophisticated. There is, however, little about
the house to interest the home craftsman, so it is not illustrated. Its most interesting feature, giving a hint of family dissension on the distaff side, is the superb
scenic block-printed paper which was discovered by a recent owner under
many layers of wallpaper of the baser and more modern sort. Jacob's wife may
have had an understandable scorn of her brother-in-law's difficulty with the
wandering "artist" as well as pride of possession of the real thing. Today, we
cannot understand how such splendor could have been hidden from view.
Truly, "there is no accounting for taste."

These two houses, both of Group One, have hardly been changed from the
days when the workmen packed up their tools and left. Over on the other side
of the Green Mountains the Robinson House, previously mentioned, is even
more interesting than that of Jonas Galusha because its germ, the "first little
house," was larger and finer and had its addition made during the lifetime of
the first owner. Scattered shreds of legend to which are added strands of archi-

7: ROBINSON HOUSE, SOUTH READING
One of Ebenezer's mantels

tectural evidence weave a fabric slightly colored by imagination and held together by a few authentic dates.

Ebenezer Robinson fought in the Revolution. Like many other soldiers he was discharged in Vermont's Champlain Valley, far from his distant home. A good woodsman, he threaded his way afoot through the wilderness, subsisting on the abundant small game and sleeping under the trees of the forest, seeking the Connecticut River where he knew there were trails and settlements and help in getting back to his home.

Late one afternoon, still a good day's tramp from the river, he made camp in an especially sightly place. The ground fell towards the east. A wide panorama spread before him, the dome of Mt. Ascutney in the distance. A farmer, he noted

8: ROBINSON HOUSE, SOUTH READING
Ebenezer's "new" house

that the soil was fertile and could be made into good farmland with a little work. *Here* was the place for a new home!

In due time he got his grant of land, an important part of a soldier's pay, and on it he built a log cabin, a temporary shelter. He cleared and sowed a couple of fields, and the crop looked promising. He then made the long journey back to his old home and brought his wife and all their possessions up to the new one. Progress was slow over the rough wilderness trail with the ox-drawn cart so heavily laden, but its hardships were forgotten in the joy of the young couple as they reached the new place at last.

It is amazing that a man clearing new land and farming under the difficulties of working without modern labor-saving machinery had any *spare* time, but in a few years—doubtless with the help of neighbors—he built a seemly story-and-a-half house for his growing family. This was finished in 1792. It had a big central chimney with three fireplaces serving the three clustering rooms.

The three mantels which Ebenezer built with his own hands are in good condition today. They bespeak the character of the man in their artless certainty of design, their charm of proportion. Figure 7 shows one of them. The wide boards that flank the fireplace were made from giant pine trees that grew on his place. Robinson prospered. He deserved success. In 1824 he built an addition, what he called "a fair mansion," the first house becoming its ell. He was a moneyed man now, with a position in the growing settlement to maintain. Although a modest man, he felt he ought to give concrete expression to his success. Oh, not too loudly.

"I'm getting old. Of course I've got to hire a good master builder. I've worked hard all my life. Time I took it easier. Folks speak well of that young Emerson. He's got to help me, tell me what we ought to do, but I'll help *him*.

"Keep the old house, of course. Kinda like it. Made the mantels myself, one winter. What a job the boys and I had working up those big old pines! Guess my woman's right; want something more modern in the new house. Ought to be just a mite fancier. He'll know, it's what I'm paying him for."

And so the new house came into being. It is a lovely one, well proportioned (Fig. 8). The old house, now the ell, fits it like a glove. There is a fine doorway facing the road, a Palladian window above it. The new main staircase is simple, but good. Some of the old stencil work remained on one of the plastered walls, hidden under the wallpaper (Fig. 58), and is interesting enough to have been used as an illustration in a recent book on the subject. The new house has four fireplaces, two on each floor. The mantels are very obviously not Robinson's work, but that of his busy housewright who had little time to make different designs. All four are nearly alike, with slight differences in their very ingenious and original details. They look "shopmade" from a stock design, but Ebenezer may have cut the details (illustrated in Chapter IX, Figs. 115, 117, at a large scale) to give them a bit of individuality. He was a good craftsman, and one may imagine his feelings when he saw them in place (Fig. 9).

" Funny, the way the end of that mantel shelf sticks out in the air. Could

9: ROBINSON HOUSE, SOUTH READING
One of the "new" bedroom mantels

hit your head on that when you reached down for a stick of wood. Doesn't look as if he's measured right. And I wonder why he didn't put a cornice at the top? Could've shortened those pilasters that much. Mebbe he knows best. Anyway, they're new style. That'll please the woman."

The old house emerges from the mists of the past in 1948 when it was bought and intelligently restored by the couple mentioned early in this chapter. It was a much more difficult operation than many others. It needed skilled help to re-place old rotted sills and beams. The rebuilding of the chimney, described in Chapter VII, was in itself an ingenious and expensive piece of work. The stenciling was saved and carefully copied, matching the old colors. Very wisely, the operations were not hurried, but carried out slowly, a little at a time. Old sash were repaired where possible and replaced where necessary by others taken from a neighboring ruinous building which also furnished some needed wide floor boards. They were lucky enough to find Ebenezer's old cobbler's bench which he had used for so many years, repairing the family's shoes. They even discovered its original place by scars in the worn floor boards, close to one of the hearths. It was a happy experience for all concerned, and the enthusiasm of the owners was shared by their workmen. They all felt they really knew old Mr. Robinson by the time the restoration was completed.

Perhaps few home craftsmen would dare tackle as big and expensive a job as that. On the other hand, few of the old houses that people buy need as much reconstruction as this one. It was more rewarding than anyone can imagine— until they try it. They will discover new pleasures, though, in working on an old house with their own hands and realize that they have made an investment that pays unexpected dividends, even if they are intangibles.

A word of caution to the seeker for "a little place in the country." The view, at the time of your first visit, may have been entrancing. The house is obviously charming and one's fingers itch to make the needed repairs or restorations. But what about the water supply? At the time the house was built, perhaps it was served by a never-failing spring. Since then the protective forest may have been cut down, leaving the present flow of water a seasonal one. This has hap-pened. In old times houses had no plumbing other than a kitchen sink, and people took baths only once a week. They did not sprinkle lawns nor water the vegetable and flower gardens. Even if their water supply was ample for them, and has not diminished with the passing years, it may be insufficent for present-day requirements.

Suppose the spring *does* hold up through a drought that the old timers say is the worst in their memory; will the water be ruled potable when a sample is given to the State Board of Health? If the supply is from a well instead of a spring, it may be polluted from a barnyard, long deserted, where manure has soaked the ground from which the well gets its flow. A deep "artesian" well may be the solution, but the depth to which it has to be drilled is always a gamble. The purchaser of an old farm in a Pennsylvania valley, finding his ample spring not potable, drilled a deep well only to learn that the farm half a mile away on the slope above him in that limestone country was polluting his new drilled well. Before buying an old place with a possible outlay of several thousand dollars, it may be wise to have a test-well driven at a small fraction of the later investment.

If the water supply is ample and pure, there is also the problem of sewage disposal. This means a septic tank of a size to care for the number of persons who are to live in the house. This must drain into a properly designed filter bed which will purify the outflow of the septic tank so it does not pollute the present water supply. The outflow of a septic tank is *not* pure water, as too many persons think, but merely liquified sewage. An adequate filter bed is a necessity.

The ancient proverb that "Difficulties show what men are" may give encouragement, but "Look before you, ere you leap" urges precaution.

[II]

THE WAY THEY BUILT

————◆•◉•◆————

AN OUTLINE of old-time methods of house construction is valuable and pertinent even if this book deals chiefly with architectural details. The present owner of a Colonial house can plan alterations more wisely if he has even a slight knowledge of the old ways of building and their basic differences from present-day practise.

All Early American wooden houses were of the traditional framed construction; the brick ones varied only in their outside walls. The timbers were massive and hand-hewn, their sizes determined by experience, "by guess and by gosh," for engineering laboratories to determine strength of materials and advise "safe loads" in tabular form were still half a century away. True, the hand-hewn beams were wasteful of wood as we know now, but they pleased the eye. They *looked* strong enough, and we still find them good to look at. They are worthy of admiration, sometimes of being exposed to view. These old hand-hewn timbers were joined together *without nails* by various joints, accurately cut, and secured by big wooden pins called "trunnels" (tree nails). This construction was amazingly rigid. There are cases of such a house being swept downstream in a flood, hauled out from its grounding place by yokes of oxen, moved on rollers to a new foundation, and continuing as a comfortable dwelling!

The lowest members of the frame, and the most important, are the sills. These are big timbers, set flatways on the foundation walls. Anyone buying an old house should inspect its foundations carefully, as they might be a source of future trouble, usually settlement, causing distortion of the frame. Probably they were built with suitable footings, far enough below frost line to prevent heaving, or their deficiency would have shown up long ago in floors now far from level. Possibly they were built of stone laid "dry," that is, without mortar. Many such walls were so skilfully built that today they are in better condition than newer walls, poorly laid with rougher stones and held together only by mortar which is now failing. Yet a "dry wall" may leak air and water. It can be bettered by pointing, filling the exposed joints with cement mortar, which would add nothing to the strength of the wall but would make it tight.

In the case of wings or ells that have no cellars, it is wise to dig exploratory holes outside to determine the depth of the foundations and their condition, if there is no crawl hole giving access from the cellar of the main house to the space under the floor of the wing.

If foundation walls are found partly in bad condition, they may be made secure without going to the considerable expense of rebuilding the unsatisfactory part by casting a concrete wall against it, of adequate thickness, tapering from a wide bottom to a narrower top. This should start a little deeper than the top of the cellar floor. These operations are better done by professionals rather than by an amateur owner.

Sills are easily tested for soundness by attempting to thrust the blade of a pocket knife in them. Rot may be due to an easily stopped leak that may have been neglected for years, or to "dry rot" caused by inadequate ventilation of the cellar. Repairs are essential. An experienced man can suggest ways to do the job cheaply.

The floors are supported by heavy beams, set a good deal farther apart than is the modern custom. Those of the ground floor are not always hewn square. They may be merely flattened on top to receive the floor boards. Usually one end of the beam is framed into the sill (the corresponding timber on the second floor is called a summer beam), and the other end into a big girder, its length usually the whole width of the house. This is not necessarily a single stick, but the joint should be made over a column, preferably of masonry set in mortar, if it is a ground-floor timber. Those on the second floor rest on heavy hewn posts and their load is, of course, carried down to the cellar pier or sills. The floor beams are framed into the girders, or the sills of the outside wall, with mortise-and-tenon joints. The mortise is a rectangular hole cut into the supporting timber. The tenon, a sort of tongue on the ends of the beams, fits tightly into the mortise. The depth of the girder is usually more than that of the beams it carries, and it generally is much wider than the beams, a really big fellow.

Second-floor construction is similar, but its beams and girders are usually smoothly hewn so that they might be exposed to view on the ground-floor ceilings. Generally the ceilings were plastered over "to look better" in later and more prosperous years. Tastes have changed.

Obviously the weight of the ground-floor timbers (dead load) and the people and furniture (live load) is carried by the sills directly to the foundation walls and cellar piers. That of the second floor, attic, and roof is concentrated by the long roof plates and summer beams on the big corner posts and probably some intermediate ones. These are the chief and great differences between framed construction and the modern way of building. Today's floor loads are distributed between the stud walls of the exterior and the "bearing" stud partitions of the *interior*. In the oldest buildings there were no exterior studs. The plank walls had little to do beside carry the trivial weights of clapboards and plaster, doors and windows. The huge corner posts, taking their loads from the summer beams and the plates, which are the top horizontal members of the frame that carry the rafters and attic-floor beams, were usually visible, projecting into the rooms. Sometimes they had rather short diagonal braces framed into their sides and to the summer beams or plates, to stiffen the structure. The end product is a building that with ordinary care has a life expectancy of several hundred years.

One may remember from childhood days building a house of cards and the way two cards, set up in A-shape, would collapse if their bottoms were on a shiny table instead of a cloth. Rafters have the same tendency under the dead load of their own weight, plus that of the roof covering, and snow, to which is added the very considerable live load of gale winds. The rafters are held at the top by the big ridge beam into which they are framed. This is often an odd pentagonal shape in cross section, the two top sides matching the slope of the roof boards, the lower sides at right angles to them, and the bottom flat. The lower ends of the rafters frame into the plate. Even a sturdy plate might bulge out with all this load, but the attic floor beams, which are framed into the plate on each side of the house, the joints being pinned, tie the whole together. Careful fitting, accurate joints, trunnels driven into neatly bored holes at the proper points, make a framed house very much more rigid than a modern one—and not a nail in the framing!

Partitions in the really old houses were placed at will and, like the outside walls at that time, were made of solid two-inch planks set on end, secured to the frame at top and bottom. Usually they were plastered. Occasionally the planks were planed smooth and exposed to view, as shown in Figure 7. They either had tight joints, or some sort of device so they fitted into one another, such as a tongue-and-groove or an overlap. Very rarely this joint had a small moulding planed on the edge. Unfortunately for us, the introduction of wallpaper at low prices, around 1840, resulted in plastering over many existing decorative plank walls to make a smooth surface to take the paper. Before that time it was done so the walls might have decorative painted stencil work, bringing a bit of color into an austere interior, like that in Ebenezer Robinson's house (Fig. 85).

What may be called "middle-aged" houses did not have plank walls, either on the outside or as partitions, but stud walls, quite like our modern ones except that they were not always used as bearing walls as was the case later. Sometimes these studs were hewn, four inches thick and wide but set farther apart than our present standard of sixteen inches. Plank walls are, of course, solid. They give no space for concealed wires and piping as do today's hollow stud walls, but they permit the modern owner to change their position, or to remove them altogether, because they carry no load.

Flooring methods and material changed little from pre-Revolutionary times to the Civil War period. Floor boards were thicker than today, as would be natural with beams spaced more widely. Most of them are about 1 1/8 inches thick, rough on the under side, and the top and edges dressed so they might be set close together. Clear white pine was the favored material, and there was a marked preference for wide boards, although few floors show the boards all of the same width. The attic, a modern source of old boards for replacement, was usually floored with culls. Those culls today are eagerly removed for use as they have borne little traffic, while some of the ground-floor boards had been replaced with less desirable material years ago.

Roof and floor boards were secured by hand-wrought nails driven into the rafters or beams—the only use of iron in the house, with the exception of the necessary hinges, latches, and bolts. These nails, of several sizes according to their use, were made by the local blacksmith, who had plenty of work to do besides making and applying shoes for horses and oxen. Shoeing was almost a side line. In more closely settled places, there were small factories for nail-making before this was taken over by machines. The first machine-made nails, stamped out of thick sheets of iron, were called "cut nails." They were in common use from about 1840 until about fifty years later, when they were super-seded by the steel-wire nails used today. These come in a bewildering variety of lengths, body and heads, and a house builder now uses many different sizes and kinds.

In old houses with their square-edged boards, the nail heads showed and were not very sightly. Being hard, they gave a certain amount of protection to the softwood floor immediately around them so it did not wear away with traffic as fast as other parts of the boards. This sometimes made it difficult to get a level area for table or chair legs. In the more costly homes, the places where the nails were to be driven were "counter-bored," that is, a half-inch hole was bored to a similar depth, the nail driven through the center of the hole, which was then plugged with a circular piece of wood, giving the effect of the head of a wooden peg. This wore at the same rate as the rest of the floor, and insured a level surface. Nothing could be done, however, to prevent the cracks between the square-edged boards from opening a little in weather when the humidity was abnormally low. Small objects like coins might drop through these cracks and be lost. Worse yet, because the boards were in only one layer, cold air from the cellar was drawn up by the draft requirements of the open fires. That explains the prevalence of footstools (sometimes called crickets) in old times. Our ancestors, as they sat in their chairs, did not have unusually short legs. They had cold feet. The cure was to keep them off the drafty floor!

With the Machine Age came a good many comforts. Flooring as used today may not be as sightly as the wide old boards, but our narrow strips are tongued-and-grooved, and the wire nails are not driven through the top surface of the floor board but are concealed, "blind nailed," so there are no visible nails or cracks and no drafts. Modern floors are warmer also because they are double. That is, there is a rough or under floor, generally laid diagonally instead of at right angles to the beams, covered with building paper or a sort of felt, on which the finish floor is laid. The old floors were always single thickness.

From pre-Revolutionary days down to the present the outside walls have been covered with clapboards, wedge shaped in cross section and nailed through the upper edges so succeeding courses cover and protect the nails. These require painting, and repainting every few years. It seems odd that they were used so much instead of shingles, which need no paint. In the very old houses the paint was a homemade "barn red," very durable and, as the pigment perhaps might be dug in the neighborhood, cheap. White oil paint had to be bought. Lime whitewash, also homemade, was not at all durable.

None of the lumber used could be bought at a local mill, as it is today. The farmer-owner went out into his wood lot and selected the trees and felled them. This was generally done in winter, when the sap was down and the tree dormant. He trimmed off the limbs, then sawed the big trunks into logs long enough for the purposes he had in mind. One at a time, his patient oxen snaked them downhill through the snow to the skidway where they were stacked. Later, while sledding was still good, he would yoke his team to a sledge, get a good load on it, and draw the logs down to the site of the new house. There they would lie to season or dry out, maybe for a year, often stripped of bark. These were usually softwood logs. Occasionally maple was used, but while it lasts forever, it is heavy stuff. Fewer logs make a load, and it needs a lot more work to ready them for use. Pine was a favorite wood, perhaps next to spruce, which is supposed to resist decay longer than most woods. If his wood lot was in the lower altitudes, he presumably had plenty of hemlock, not as strong or lasting as the others, but its bark could give him a by-product to sell to the local tannery if he didn't want to use it at home. His work in the woods was done in winter. It was hard work for man and beast, but the man had a chance to have the delight of accomplishment. A person who has not worked in the woods in winter cannot quite understand how enjoyable it can be.

City people come to Vermont for winter sports, driving in easy-riding heated cars over well-plowed highways. Then they and their skis are taken up to the top of a hill by machine-powered lifts. They glide swiftly down and repeat it for hours, with refreshment breaks in jolly company. Of course it is fun. But the pioneer went out on foot, breaking trail with his snowshoes through deep, powdery snow, breathing lungfuls of cold and invigorating air full of fragrance. As he went he studied trails in the snow—a lynx after a big rabbit or a circular scar on the smooth surface, bloodied where a hungry owl had got his meal of partridge. When he paused in his chopping to rest a bit he could let his eyes rove over *his* woodland, get glimpses of *his* snow-covered fields far below, blue sky and white clouds above. He was doing hard work and quietly exulted in his skill. Lunch time came and he sat on a log, after he had baited his oxen with hay from the homespun sacks they had brought up on their backs. He opened his lunch; home-baked bread, butter from his cows, smoked ham from his pigs. Thirsty, he broke the ice on a pool in the brook and got a good long drink, then led his oxen over for theirs. It was a good life.

Another day, down at home, he started work on his logs, now well seasoned by their year in sun and rain. With his razor-sharp axe he made stop cuts, then, with slanting blows, hewed the log square, one side at a time. This was followed by smoothing with the broadaxe, a mighty weapon, its blade something like that of the usual axe but the cutting edge about a foot long and the helve rather short, straight instead of curved. This removed much of the rough-hewn surface and might finish the job in most cases. If he wanted an especially fine piece of work, as for an exposed ceiling beam, he then used an adze, a most dangerous tool in the hands of any but an expert. The blade is set at right angles to the usual axhead, like a wicked sort of hoe, its edge about the same width as that of an axe, and very, very sharp. Its long helve is straight. He straddled the squared beam and, slowly chopping between his legs, shaved its slightly rough surface down to what he wanted. It might be almost as smooth as if planed, but the surface showed, in the right light, a gentle waviness that no machine can duplicate. Few indeed are the new owners, admiring their beamed ceiling, who realize the labor that went into those timbers.

The circular saw was invented at the end of the eighteenth century. In those far-off days before electric motors, its use was limited to mills with water power, so for several decades hewn timbers were used if they were big ones. Indeed, many Vermont water-powered sawmills did not get a circular saw until well into the 1850's. Even if the nearest mill did have a circular saw it might be so far away from the home site that the time and cost of hauling logs over the crude roads of those days, and back again, would make hand-hewing cheaper and quicker. The older mills sawed big logs with an up-and-down saw, a long blade that rose and fell by an ingenious transfer of power from the water wheel's revolving shaft by means of cranks. It is easy to tell from the saw marks on old timbers which kind of saw was used in cutting them. The up-and-down saw leaves parallel marks on the wood; the circular saw, concentric curved ones.

In old times boards cost more, relatively, than rough-hewn framing timbers. Today, the old boards have a very different value, a historical one, for if they came from a mill they show what kind of saw had cut them. Historians are often able to determine from them dates otherwise unobtainable.

If logs were cut into boards at home the work was done by hand in a saw pit. This was a kind of well dug in the ground with a staging over it on which the log might be moved as required. One man was down in the pit, the other straddling the log, above. The saw was a long-bladed one, not too different from today's two-man saw used to crosscut logs in the woods, except that its handles were set at right angles to the blade. It took great skill to saw a board so it would be perfectly straight from end to end and also of the same thickness throughout its length. Thin boards, with their tendency to wabble as they were cut from the log, were much more difficult to produce. That is why the more easily made planks two or three inches thick were used for partitions and elsewhere. Mills, replacing men with water power, could do the job faster as well as more accurately. It was cruelly hard work to pump that saw up and down and keep it cutting truly too! This explains why there are many houses in which the big main timbers are hewn, even if the floor beams and rafters are sawed. They may have been cheaper in the end although the thinner sawed timbers had to be spaced closer together in order to carry their loads, so more of them were needed. This mixture of hand and machine work began about 1850 and was common up to the time of the Civil War. Wood was still relatively cheap, so rafters and floor beams, smaller than the hewn ones, were usually three inches thick instead of today's standard two inches.

It was about this time, when the Colonial style became dormant, that timber sizes grew smaller while retaining their old designations. As late as 1880, for example, a two-by-four was two inches thick and four inches wide as would be expected. How these dimensions have shrunk! Today, this commonest size of construction lumber has been standardized at only 1 5/8 inches thick and 3 5/8 inches wide. Truly, "skim milk masquerades as cream." These nominal but dwindling sizes are customary in the larger timbers too, so the engineering tables

10: HARRIS HOUSE, CASTLETON
A typical Colonial house

giving "safe loads" for various conditions have had to be revised. Translating these shrinkages into yard goods, what drygoods salesman could get away with selling a yard of silk that was only 28 3/4 inches long? Such facts, and the knowledge that the wood used in the old houses was not only better seasoned than any in present-day markets but also of higher grade, makes an old house, if in reasonably good physical condition, an excellent investment. Its gradual embellishment will pay unexpected if intangible dividends, especially if done by the owner's hands.

Changes in lumber sizes were only one of the many symptoms of the new Machine Age, a social revolution that brought us many good things, but, like all revolutions, some that were deplorable. The farmer of the 1810's went into

11: CAMBRIDGE HOUSE, GRAFTON
The gable end faces the street

12: MATTISON HOUSE, BENNINGTON
Symmetrical end composition

13: DR. ARNOLD HOUSE, LONDONDERRY
Two "fronts" and a long ell

his own wood lots and by clearing land made new fields to cultivate, the lumber
for his home being a by-product, material that was used instead of wasted.
When railroads came to Vermont in the 1850's his woods gave him a cash crop
for the first time. He sold his logs and had some sawed for construction, using
smaller timbers. The old framed construction evolved slowly to a method in
which few members were over two inches thick. Sizes of timbers were skimped
at the expense of durability. All over the world, in this period, the standards of
good taste dropped also, as evidenced in architecture and the other arts. The
feeling for good proportion, so unfailing at the beginning of the nineteenth
century, was lost. Houses built from the 1860's on, inferior in construction and

materials, are not always a good buy. There are exceptions, but caution and close inspection are desirable.

Oddly enough, with all the various abandonments of old ways, the early Colonial house *plan* persisted. It consists of a rectangle whose sides are longer than the ends. Within this is a central hall of generous width with two rooms on each side. This is expressed on the exterior by the grouping of openings, as shown in Figure 10, from which it is apparent that the second-floor plan is practically the same. In the typical building the main entrance is in the middle of the long part of the rectangle, which therefore becomes the front of the house. This is the usual arrangement for all free-standing buildings, but in villages, due to the smaller area on which the house must be erected, the typical rectangle must be turned so that the gable end faces the street. Generally, the village house is not as wide as one in the country. The interior plan must change, so the entrance door, hall, and staircase are on one side. The composition then becomes an unsymmetrical one, and it is more important that the doorway be considerably embellished as shown in Figure 11. Chapter IV suggests ways of doing this where required.

In those houses set with the gable end facing the road or street and large enough to permit the entrance to be in the middle, it becomes the focus of a dignified and symmetrical composition. An example is shown in Figure 12. Obviously this requires a larger building lot than is found in most cases, in a village.

Occasionally, old houses were built with important entrances on both the gable end and the side. Most of these were originally taverns or inns, but Figure 13 shows one that was erected by a physician in 1810, close to a small river in a sprawling little village. One door is supposed to have led into his "surgery" with its waiting room, but tradition is silent about the third handsome doorway in the two-story ell, itself a curiosity because it has two full floors. Possibly at some time another house was moved to this new location, to make the building into a "tenement," as multiple dwellings are called in Vermont.

Few of the really old houses have come down to us in their original simple rectangular plan. Most of them have had additions, a wing or an ell. In very old houses this little structure may be the original home, and as family and wealth

14: WHITTON HOUSE, EAST POULTNEY
A gabled end between two wings

increased, the "new house" attached to it became the main building, a case of the tail wagging the dog, historically. Sometimes these annexes are decrepit and a new owner wants to better them. Perhaps a brand new one is wanted and suggestions in the following text and illustrations may help solve some of the problems that will arise.

The two names, wing and ell, are not synonymous, nor are the desirable architectural treatments the same. A wing is an addition with its length running the same way as that of the house, and is attached at the *end* of the house, sometimes with its middle or axis in continuation of that of the house, or, quite as often, set back from it. In some of the Greek Revival homes there are wings of similar design symmetrically placed at each end, while the main body of the house is set with its gable end forming the front and columned like a Greek

15: BRICK FARMHOUSE, ARLINGTON
Gambrel and gable roofs

temple. As a monumental structure it adds considerably to the dignity of the village street (Figure 14) even if it is so small. As a practical dwelling it could be a constant source of irritation to its inmates. A Greek temple was eminently successful for its function, but the needs of a dwelling are fundamentally different, and it is hard to understand why a hard-headed Vermonter ever tried to reconcile such diametrically opposite requirements.

In many cases circumstances made additions necessary. If the family became more affluent, the first simple dwelling became either the ell (Fig. 8) to which the new and larger house was attached, or, quite as often, a wing of the new. An interesting exception to this sequence is seen in Figure 15. Here the original gambrel-roofed brick house was found too small by a later owner who added a gabled wooden wing. It will be conceded that it is a complete success. Nevertheless, if a new owner wants to add a wing to an existing building he will be wise if he designs it in harmony with the old work, both in style and material.

Normally the wing was considerably shorter than the house, as suggested by good proportion. In many parts of New England where the snowfall is heavy, sometimes burying all fences completely, the ell or wing was greatly lengthened, ending with one or more of the barns. A recent author has called this "continuous architecture," a vivid phrase. For example, there is a certain big farmhouse built around 1810 in Orleans County, Vermont. Its story-and-a-half wing holds a big kitchen, the pantries, and the milkroom. Beyond this it is extended, under the same roof, to include a big woodshed, a driveway passage for loaded hay wagons to pass through, a farm workshop, the carriage house, the henhouse. Then comes the roomy cowshed which forms one end of the big barnyard, and finally attaches to the huge barn with its stanchions for the cattle, a granary and an enormous hay storage space. The total length of that wing is several times longer than the house.

A similar example shown in Figure 16 has a story-and-a-half wing with seven arched open bays reaching all the way to the barns. Those nearest the house formed a recessed porch behind which was the kitchen and its appurtenances, then followed other functional rooms and sheds to the barns. Overhead, instead of possible bedrooms, was a long loft in which the builder of the house and some of his descendants carried on the peculiar and now defunct home industry of raising silkworms. These produced a profitable quantity of raw silk having a ready sale in those days. A succession of unusually cold winters killed all the mulberry trees, whose leaves were essential to the diet of the worms, and the odd industry came to a sudden end. Now, the house itself is gone, submerged under a great new lake formed by one of the flood-control dams. Although this design is obviously an exaggeration of a good idea, it contains a suggestion for those who may need to add a long wing for similarly varied uses to a Colonial-style house.

The addition of space to a house is dictated largely by the site. If it is level, the choice between wing and ell may be affected by other factors, such as existing trees that it would be a pity to remove. The differing characters of wing and ell may help the final decision.

An ell is added to the long *side* of a building and its length runs at right angles

16: WARREN-MAXWELL FARM, WEATHERSFIELD
A brick house with a long wooden ell

to the house. The resulting shape of the completed structure is much like a capital "L," which of course is the origin of the name. While it is true that if the dwelling is on a level site there is no structural reason for choice between wing and ell, it is equally apparent that if the land is level behind the house but falls more or less steeply at its ends, an ell is the easiest way to secure added floor space. Beyond that is the matter of appearance. Wings need enough formality, or even ornamentation, to harmonize with the design of the front of the house. The ends of the house may be more or less formal, but are seldom ornate, while the back of the house is strictly utilitarian and informal. The ell naturally follows this appearance, yet retains a little of the architectural feeling of the adjoining end of the house. Figure 17 shows a successful solution of the design problem—the junction of a very plain ell with a modestly ornate house.

17: KELLOG HOUSE, BENSON
A fine house and a plain ell

This seems to have been built as a part of the original structure in 1826, the recessed porch with its delicately curved arch making a satisfactory transition which would be more evident if the modern fly screening gave a better view of the kitchen entrance and adjoining windows. The old terrace shows that the builder had to do some grading. The bow window helps too; modern, but an improvement. The typical ell is about as scarce as the average man, and for that reason a modern ell may be easier to design to harmonize with the main building.

So far, this chapter has confined itself almost entirely to the methods of building, including design, of those houses erected between 1800 and about 1850. As has been pointed out, a large part of the work was done then by hand, manual labor being supplanted only by the power-operated circular saw. Slowly, very

slowly, new inventions came into use and a gradual change began, a little before 1850, that increased to what may be termed an architectural revolution.
A great number of new things came into common use without which we would
not and should not get on today. Of these the stove made the greatest change in
both the plan and the appearance of dwellings, due to the disuse and, in the
case of new houses, the omission of open fireplaces, with their mantels. This
loss shifted, almost eliminated, the focus of a room. On the exterior, the smaller
chimneys required by stoves made a notable change in appearance (discussed
in Chapter VII). Modern plumbing was introduced, which altered the house
plan by requiring a bathroom.

The sad thing about this revolution, adding a corroding acid to the increasing
ease and softness of life, was the marked decadence of good taste to which reference has already been made. Perhaps some philosopher of the next century
will give a valid explanation for this. There is no apparent reason why a
machine-made door or window sash should not be of lovely proportions, as the
old ones were. Fortunately, the wheel is turning and some of today's machine-
made doors and windows can scarcely be told from the best ones of 1830.
A minor example, but significant.

The most encouraging development is the increasing popular interest in good
architecture. People are beginning to recognize that excellence of design may be
completely nullified by inappropriateness. A beautiful wild flower growing in
the garden's bean row is a *weed*. Perhaps that homely simile can be adapted to
design, and a victory will be won.

If this chapter has made clear the fundamental importance of the construction of a Colonial house, those that follow may prove more helpful in the restoration of some sturdy old dwelling still standing among New England's unchang-
ing hills.

18: FRENCH-HARD HOUSE, MANCHESTER
Typical hipped roof

[III]

EAVES, GABLES, AND CORNERS

———◆•◉•◆———

EAVES and gables are parts of a roof. Architects are sometimes amazed that persons who have lived under a roof for so large a part of their lives do not know the names of the different kinds of roofs that cover familiar buildings, nor their parts. Comprehension of these ancient terms that have come down to us from Saxon days is useful and may be important. The following definitions may clarify the rest of this chapter.

The flat roof, such as seen on factory buildings and many city houses, explains itself. It is a plane or flat surface which is not quite horizontal, but slopes just enough for rain water to run off. It has a close relative, the shed roof, most often seen on country houses covering a piazza. This, too, is a plane which is set with one edge against the house and the other over the porch posts, sloping at a considerable angle as chosen by the builder for the best appearance. It gets its name from being the usual roof of a cowshed or wagon shed.

The gable roof is the kind most often seen in the country on dwellings, barns, and other outbuildings (Fig. 11). Like the shed roof, the slope or pitch is a matter of taste and conformity to the style of architecture. The Victorian "Gothick" houses had very steep roofs. Snow cannot lie on them, but this is not always an advantage. If a gable roof on a dwelling is over a well-insulated attic, the slope probably will be flat enough so snow will *not* slide off under normal conditions, as it would from a steeper roof, perhaps to the detriment of the man waiting to be let in the front door. Snow makes an excellent insulator, adding to the efficiency of commercial insulation.

The overhang of the roof, where it starts sloping up from the wall of the house, is called the eaves. The sloping roofs on the two sides of the house meet at the top in the ridge, where the ends of the roof covering (slate or shingles) are protected against the weather by a ridge roll of metal, copper being the most enduring.

The parts of the roof that show on the ends of the house form a triangular space, the gable (Fig. 13), which, like the eaves, generally projects slightly from the wall of the house. A drawback of the gabled roof, if made with the usual low pitch, is the lack of useful space in the attic, due to insufficient headroom. This is not true in the larger houses, or those with a steep roof pitch. Some of the old taverns used the attic as a ballroom. The seats for the "wallflowers" were built along the low sides of the room, which often had an arched ceiling.

The gambrel roof was developed from the simpler gabled one in an effort to get usable space under the roof. In this, the roof slope starts up steeply from the eaves, and at a convenient ceiling height the slope changes abruptly to a much flatter pitch, which continues to the ridge. This type of roof was used more often in seventeenth- and eighteenth-century houses than later and is seldom found in Vermont. It gives a good deal of space for bedrooms, which may gain their light from dormer windows. Figure 15 shows a very charming old house on which are both gabled and gambrel roofs, with dormer windows best adapted to each, which are excellent in scale and placement.

An adaptation of the ancient gambrel roof was devised by a French architect, Mansard, in the seventeenth century and was very popular in his country. It was used in ours only in Victorian times. Fortunately, there are not many examples in Vermont of this inappropriate style.

The hipped roof is pyramidal in shape. The roofs of all four sides of the house slope up from their eaves at the same pitch or angle, to meet in a short ridge, its length dependent on the proportions of the rectangular plan of the house (Fig. 18). The junctions of these four slopes are called hips, and in order to keep them tight against leakage are often protected by metal rolls in the same way as the ridge. The hipped roof has few advantages from the housewright's viewpoint. The heavy timbers that form the hips complicate framing and as the rafters differ in length, each one must be cut and fitted individually. The angle of slope, if it is too steep, may overwhelm the mass of the house and if not steep enough, the roof will be invisible from near by. From the owner's point of view

19: YOUNG HOUSE, ARLINGTON
Simple cornice and return

it is undesirable as the attic cannot be lighted at all and has little storage space. But it is very good looking—perhaps that is its sole virtue.

The eaves provide an obvious place for embellishment with a wide variety of treatments that may greatly improve the looks of a plain house. Some of these are simple enough to be done by anyone handy with tools, if he does not mind working high above the ground. Others require considerable skill. Perhaps the projecting ends of the rafters are merely covered with a board to protect the absorbent end-grain from moisture. Between this board and the wall the rafters show. The effect is utterly commonplace. The cure is to make a cornice, as simple or as elaborate as desired. Figure 19 shows the utmost in simplicity. Instead of mouldings, narrow flat boards are used to form a simple and ingenious one. This is mitered at the corner to make a short "return," with the cornice carried up the gable, its lower end resting on the top of the return. Under the cornice is a wider board, a sort of frieze (to use the technical name) before the clapboards begin. Similar boards clasp the corner of the house and receive the ends of the clapboards. The result is to give a finish to that part of the building,

20: OLD DEMING TAVERN, ARLINGTON
Moulded cornice and return

21: LABATT HOUSE, ARLINGTON
Cornice, frieze, and architrave

22: HARRIS HOUSE, CASTLETON
Classical entablature

to lift it above the commonplace at small expense. Note the "return" especially in this and the following illustrations. It is an important decoration.

Figure 20 illustrates a further development, an elaboration of the scheme, by using mouldings in the cornice and bringing it closer to the Classical form that is described later. The picture also shows a pleasing enrichment of the corner boards—small mouldings at their sides making a tall thin panel out of an otherwise plain board. In Figure 21 is a treatment that is still nearer to the Classical formula, for beneath the plain board or frieze of the return there is a small unit, an architrave, made of a board to which a simple little strip of wood is added, the square edges casting pleasing shadows. The gable lacks this. Such work is easy to copy and it does an amazing amount towards improving a plain building.

The amount that gable and eaves overhang is largely a matter of taste, even when using a supposedly Classical entablature. In very old houses, those built before 1800, there is often no overhang at the gable ends, especially in little one-story dwellings. Their eaves, however, always overhang a small amount, to keep the drip of rainwater and melting snow away from the foundations. The need for this is obvious when one remembers that in these small old dwellings the foundation walls were frequently laid without mortar. We moderns like the eaves projection, for it permits us to keep the top sash of our bedroom windows open on a rainy night, protected by the eaves which we, probably, have fitted with gutters and downspouts.

Unfortunately, in the days of architectural decadence, many well-planned and well-constructed dwellings were designed with exaggerated gable and eaves projection, their cornices thin and unlovely to the eye. Here is a case for structural surgery. Let the home owner and his carpenters cut back these distressing features, prune them to proper proportions, and add cornices as well as the "returns" that will shortly be described. The improvement will surprise many who are not blessed with a vision of what might be.

It is hardly possible to go on from here without again using technical terms that should be defined, which have to do with the Classical entablature worked out by Vitruvius, a famous architect of ancient Rome. He worked in marble, and the physical characteristics of wood call for greater delicacy. The scale of a New England farmhouse requires smaller mouldings than were used in a

Roman palace. His principles have filtered down through the ages, however, reaching this country through the sort of "how-to" books that were published in England in the late 1700's. Probably no Early American housewright had ever heard of Vitruvius. Few of the early master builders owned these expensive books on Classic design, but by some sort of wireless the ideas spread. The Classical orders and their modifications were considered, translated, and adapted with characteristic freedom. The almost incredibly good taste and uncanny sense of proportion shown in this process arouse our respectful admiration today.

In the limited field of this book, covering the dwellings of plain people, it seems wise to consider the forms of entablature they used. The complete version, in Colonial style, belongs to the more ornate houses. An entablature is supported by pilasters, which are flat and secured to the wall. The entablature with which we deal is a part of the fabric of the house and often rests on no more than plain corner boards which are substituted for pilasters. A column-supported entablature is uncommon, but not unknown, in Vermont.

A full entablature has three divisions. The lowest is called the architrave and is a very simple grouping of square-edged boards just above the clapboards, as shown in Figure 21. A more elaborate one, the lowest division of an ornate entablature, is illustrated in Figure 22. It is supported by the plain corner boards. In Figure 23 elaborate pilasters with bases at the bottom and capitals at the top replace the corner boards. This treatment is generally found on houses that were built in the early 1800's. Figure 24, a house built about 1855, has a peculiar entablature, without a trace of an architrave, and the twin pilasters share one capital. Such is the independence of our Vermont housewrights.

The second, or middle part of a complete entablature is called the frieze. It is a flat board which lies in the plane of the clapboards of the wall below. Frequently it is left perfectly plain, but in the more elaborate entablatures, such as are found indoors or as part of an ornate entrance feature, various ornaments may be applied to it, like the festoons that show in Figure 22 or the lozenge-shaped and floral *appliqués* in the frieze in Figure 25. These ornaments may be of carved wood nailed on or of gesso. This is a putty-like material that was pressed in moulds and when hardened, nailed in place. Gesso was a popular material for pseudo-carvings in the first part of the nineteenth century. The

23: SOULE HOUSE, FAIRFIELD
Entablature and pilaster

24: DUTTON PLACE, TOWNSHEND
Corner and gable treatments

25: MALLORY-JONES HOUSE, CASTLETON
Gable (pediment) treatment

26: PROCTOR HOUSE, PROCTORSVILLE
More amazing than admirable

true Classic triglyph, the proper thing to put in a frieze, is occasionally seen. This is a board with three V-shaped grooves cut in it. The boards are spaced far enough apart for good looks, usually with the blank space between the triglyphs at least as wide as it is high (Frontispiece).

The cornice is the top group of mouldings in the entablature, growing up and out, as it were, from the frieze. It is the most important part of the whole composition and therefore the most varied in its appearance. It is usually carried up the slope of the gable in its entirety, even if no other part of the entablature accompanies it (Figs. 19, 21). With the greater elaboration of the frieze that appears in Figures 22, 23, and 25, the cornice becomes more complicated. Its top moulding, called the cyma, has a curved cross section, usually an ogee (which is shaped like an "S"), between plain square-edged pieces. Below this is a box-like projection, the corona, important for the part it plays in the design by its high-lighted vertical face and the shadow cast on the frieze by its projection from the wall. The bed mould comes below this and forms the junction with the frieze, but there are some important variations at this point. There may be a series of modillions, which are brackets of shapes that vary greatly, as shown in Figures 23 to 25 inclusive. Rarely, in an entablature as large as that of the eaves of a house, but frequently in the smaller ones used in entrance features, the modillions are replaced by dentils, and as that means "little teeth," these are easily recognized. They show in a later chapter in Figures 36, 49, and elsewhere.

Gable treatments are of two types, influenced by the eaves design. If this is plain, with a simple cornice (especially if it includes a corona), the eaves mouldings are merely carried horizontally around the corner of the building for a short distance. This is called a return. Its length is usually twice the amount of projection from the wall plus the width of the corner board or pilaster, the measurements being taken at the top member. It is shown in Figures 19 to 21. This is a very common feature and to many seems the most pleasing way to treat a gable. It has the advantage that the clapboards of the end wall are carried all the way up to the peak, stopping against the sloping gable mouldings, which rise from its flat top.

The gable wall needs no decoration other than windows. These may light a bedroom as shown in Figure 19, a story-and-a-half building with its roof plate higher than the attic floor, so it has adequate headroom, even if the ceiling is low. If conditions do not merit such use and the attic is merely for storage, small windows will satisfy the needs of the designer, as shown in Figure 20. In the oldest houses the gable had almost no projection. It was merely outlined with a flat board nailed against the wall, the roof boards projecting a trifle beyond it.

A full entablature complicates matters by its bulk. In a large house it is too big to use merely as a return, in which case it may be carried horizontally across the entire end to join its neighbor on the other side of the house, as in Figure 25. If the entire entablature is carrried up the slope of the gable, starting from the upper surface of the horizontal one and running up to the peak (Fig. 25), it reduces this space so that if the house is a narrow one there is barely room for some device or little window as shown in Figures 17 and 25. If the house is a wide one and presumably includes usable space in the attic, such as a ball-room, there may be ample room for a handsome arched window (Fig. 16), or, if the entablature fails to follow Classical precedents completely, one or two windows may be placed for use as well as beauty, as illustrated in Figure 24. Less often, the triangle is either perfectly unadorned as in Figure 14 or contains a purely ornamental window, its sill horizontal, from which rises a semicircular or other curved sash, its muntins forming some unusual pattern, often fan-like.

The old builders occasionally tried experiments to get usable attic space, sometimes to meet an innkeeper's desire for a ballroom and sometimes for no reason that may be guessed at from history. A curious example is given in Figure 26. This is a notably ornate village residence built by a wealthy man. Like most town houses, its end faces the street, with the stables and other dependencies at the rear of what was presumably a generous lot at the time it was built. It is noteworthy for its lavish carving and decoration which could not be afforded today. The entablature, which lacks an architrave, has an elaborate interlace or network, apparently sawed from thin wood and secured to the frieze. It is so firmly fastened that in all these years since it was built in the first decade of the 1800's the condition is still perfect. The same is true of the ornament on the corona of the cornice, which bears semicircular cusps on its entire length. At the corners are piers or pilasters with curious capitals but conventional bases. The

27: MISS HALL'S HOUSE, GRAFTON
Curious but interesting

framing of the middle or hall bay is marked by similar, intermediate pilasters. A broad horizontal band indicates the location of the second floor and practically bisects the shafts of the pilasters. The lower half of each of these is fluted in Classic style, but the upper half bears an elaborate vine design carved on the solid wood. The small-paned sashes have been gone for a long time. It is a curious and amazing house and could have been almost admirable if its proportions were not crushed by the top-heavy gable. The fanlight in the gable presumably opened to a ballroom, while the little oval window in the peak gave light to a cockloft. It is a strange piece of work. Today, the well-kept edifice shown in the picture has become a tenement house and everything is sadly run down. *Sic transit*. . . .

Probably top-heavy gables offended our forebears' sense of beauty; for they tried various experiments to provide attic space. The most successful solution, of which there are a good many examples scattered around the state, is shown in Figure 27. Part of the front of the house is treated like a three-story piazza, the upper one recessed into the big gable by a deep archway. The floors are supported by big square wooden pillars, perfectly plain. This would have been ideal for an inn, which could use the top floor for a ballroom or, as is rumored was the case in the building illustrated, a Masonic lodge room. In some residences, instead of carrying the second floor out to the colonnade for an upstairs piazza a more conventional plan was to place the true front of the house at the back of the ground-floor piazza, and support the roof extension with its arched recess on a handsome row of columns. In one such dwelling the family, which had been musical for generations, used this top-floor room as the "music room." In it are two concert grand pianos and cabinets for the stringed and wood-wind instruments played by the young folks and their friends at informal concerts. The outside balcony overlooks the steep drop to the Connecticut River and enjoys a view far into the New Hampshire hills.

"Eaves, Gables, and Corners." The last group is so closely related to the other two that text and illustrations have covered most of the ground. One other corner treatment remains, however : the quoin. Essentially, it is a masonry detail. It is a visible means of bonding, or tying together, longitudinal and transverse walls that are built of brick or stone or a combination of the two. The quoin, like the lintel which carries the weight of a masonry wall over a door

28: HINSDILL HOUSE, BENNINGTON
Corner and window treatment

29: MATTISON HOUSE, BENNINGTON
Reeded pilasters

or window opening, was always of cut stone. This book does not include many houses that were built of stone or brick for two reasons. The first is that such a structure is pretty well fixed in design and is not susceptible to decoration or other change of the outside walls. The other, that masonry buildings are not common in the period covered in this book.

We like to think that the work of the old housewrights was characterized by sincerity and a dislike of shams. That is a part truth. The earliest Vermont house designs were based on the English Georgian style. Wood was scarce and costly in that country and seldom used for house building. In New England the conditions were reversed. Our Colonial style was evolved from adaptations of designs originally intended for masonry construction. It is natural that evolution should start from copying and go on to adaptation, which was just what happened, and Vermonters were a bit more independent of tradition than some of the builders in the older communities when translating stone forms into wood.

Wooden lintels, constructionally adequate for their load, were first made in imitation of the stone ones, even to the slanting, radial ends. What could have been more natural than to use the highly decorative quoins of masonry construction copied in wood, for the corners of a frame house? Fillmore used both in his design for the attractive Hinsdill House (Fig. 28). He started with corner boards of the usual thickness, but considerably wider than usual, against which the clapboards stop. The quoins, their corners beveled, are nailed to the corner boards, long and short ones alternating just as if they were stone. They give a pleasing effect, much less severe than the usual straight corner board or pilaster, and the clapboards advertise the woodenness of the house. Is this imitation of stonework insincerity? Perhaps Fillmore had twinges of conscience, for he designed the three-arched Palladian window of the house front with unusually slim casings, their arches of such slenderness that if they had been of stone, they would not have lasted through a Vermont winter. One can imagine he justified himself by saying, "No sane person would think this is a stone house, why not be a little playful in its decoration?"

There are other parts of the exterior decoration than the three of the chapter title. Some formal dwellings, perhaps deserving of being called mansions, have intermediate pilasters on the façade as well as at its corners. Often they are not merely thick, flat planks with simple cap and base, but are paneled or fluted like the corner ones that have already been shown (Fig. 86). Forming a long thin panel by nailing simple, narrow mouldings on the sides of plain pilasters or of unadorned corner boards is a simple job for any home craftsman, and if plain caps and bases are added, a marked improvement to the looks of a house may be made at very slight expense. Fluting, however, is a job for a properly equipped mill and requires new material. It is beyond the ability of most home craftsmen.

There is a third method of decorating pilasters, however, a very unusual one but effective in appearance and not too difficult to do. Few of the old-time men used it, perhaps because it was not "according to Hoyle," but the experiment was justified when tried. The scheme starts with "framing" the pilaster shaft as mentioned above but instead of mouldings using rectangular strips about three-quarters of an inch thick, or more, and about an inch wide. Instead of leaving the panel thus formed a blank space, long lengths of softwood dowel stock about an inch in diameter are nailed, side by side, inside the "frame" (Fig. 29). Something of the sort was invented by a Bennington County housewright, his name long forgotten, who used it with excellent effect in several houses. This is called "reeding." Reeded decoration of pilasters is effective and easy, while the conventional flutes cannot be added to an existing house.

[IV]

EXTERIOR WINDOWS
AND
DOORS

———◆•◉•◆———

FENESTRATION is a long word and its meaning is somewhat obscure to the layman. An architect uses it to describe the placing of door and window openings in an important wall of a building. It includes their individual proportions and inter-relationships as well as the decorative effect they have on the building as a whole, aside from any ornamentation of their casings. The old master builders had a remarkable grasp of the importance of fenestration, which is not always shared or understood by today's laymen. Probably few of them have even considered the fundamental value of these "holes in the wall" which give scale and rhythm to the composition. They do not realize that making a change in fenestration may be disastrous. *Unwise alterations* have ruined many old buildings.

New owners sometimes want to change these openings. They would profit by trying a very simple experiment, using a sheet of paper of ordinary type-writer size. Lay the paper with its long sides as top and bottom, draw lines or crease the paper about half an inch up from the bottom edge and 2 1/2 inches down from the top. The bottom line will represent the top of the stone foundation, the top being the under side of the eaves treatment and the space between them will be about the proportion of an average house-front in the old Colonial style. Then cut, from dark wrapping paper, nine little rectangles about 5/8ths of an inch wide and an inch high, for the small windows used in the oldest buildings; and nine more, for the larger, later, windows, a little less than 3/4 of an inch wide and 1 3/8 inches high. Also cut a piece of the dark paper for the door, 3/4 of an inch wide and 1 3/4 inches high. The materials for the experi-

30: DANA HOUSE, WOODSTOCK
Street front

ment are roughly at a scale in which 1/4 inch is equal to one foot at the building
and the two sets of window-pieces are about equivalent to average window
openings of the parts of the period when the best Early American houses were
built.

These may now be arranged on the white paper, bearing in mind that the
level of the ground floor will be about a 1/4 inch above the bottom crease, and
that of the second floor about 2 1/4 inches above it. The second-floor ceiling
will be a little less than two inches higher, floor thicknesses will be about 1/4
inch, walls and partitions about 1/8 inch thick.

Place the "front door" in the middle, the bottom of the dark paper at floor
level. About an inch higher will be the bottoms of the five second-floor windows,
one of which should be right over the door. Space the other four for the first

31: PERKINS-WHITE HOUSE, WEST SHAFTSBURY
East end and part of ell

trial at even distances, the outer ones about 1 7/8 inches in from the end walls. Of course, if the experiment is based on a real house, these dimensions should be changed to fit, remembering that a quarter of an inch represents twelve inches of the house. Then place the ground-floor windows. The first discovery, probably expected, is that the windows on the second floor should be directly over those on the first. The next may be that equidistant spacing of the second-floor windows gives a very uninteresting grouping. It will look much better if the outer pairs are set closer together, perhaps with the same space at the ends as that between the pairs and the middle window. Thicknesses of partitions and outside walls as well as provision of spaces for furniture may affect this, but do not waste too much time on those details. When it looks fairly well, place the ground-floor windows, their bottoms either about 5/8 of an inch above the ground floor, or with their tops on a line with that of the front door. It is obvious that the outer pairs of windows on the second floor *must* come above those on the lower one. The Colonial style is a formal one. The picturesque irregularities of romantic architecture are as out of keeping with it as brown hiking shoes would be to a man in formal evening dress.

Figure 30 shows a house with second-floor windows spaced evenly, the monotony of the front little helped by the difference in window trim of first and second floors. Compare it with Figure 18 and note the different rhythm. The first is like the monotonous beat of a drum, without accent; the second, despite the likeness of all five windows, has a marked rhythm, "boom-de-boom."

The next experiment is the most important one, for it deals with a possibly disastrous alteration, one that is sometimes very much desired: the picture window. This does not merely alter the existing rhythm, it destroys it, utterly. The effect may be demonstrated on the experimental paper by replacing one of the pairs of ground-floor windows with a single opening made by putting two of the little dark papers together, or with one slightly overlapping the other. It is apparent that the composition is wrecked, wherever this new rectangle is placed. The harmony of the entire façade is destroyed. It is as shocking as if some rowdy blew a fish-horn while a fine orchestra was playing a lovely symphony. On the paper this should be obvious. A lesson may be learned from it.

"But windows are meant to be *looked out* from," says the startled proponent, "not looked *at* from the road. There is a glorious view!" Fair enough. There may be a way, a solution. The first thing to settle is whether one big expanse of plate glass is necessary to the enjoyment of a stretch of scenery to be viewed from a living room. No landscape artist would think of painting the wide view from a mountain-top in all its breadth, as if seen from an aeroplane. He would select a part of it, framing it with nearby trees, shrubs, or rocks or more than likely find his chosen viewpoint below the summit, to provide a foreground which half-conceals, half-reveals, the beauty beyond. Ages ago women learned that a *décolletage* might be *too* extensive and that a slit skirt might make shapely limbs more attractive than shorts!

The same principle applies in architecture. The desired viewing window, instead of being an expanse of plate glass, might be a single sash of the same height as the other windows but much wider, its area being divided into small panes that might match the small panes used in the other windows. Instead of one unbroken view there would be a score of smaller ones, each one in better scale for observation, offering many delights according to the viewpoint of the observer. Artistically, then, the old mathematical dogma would be upset and the sum of the parts would be greater (in pleasure giving) than the whole. While that may be an acceptable solution for the picture window, it is not the answer for its location. While the *scale* of the wider window would harmonize with the others, its rhythm would still conflict. A rectangle that is horizontal is not in harmony with a number of vertical ones. Doubling the problem by the use of *two* such windows flanking the central entrance feature would create a discord because what is known in composition as the "void," in other words the window, would come beneath the solid walls between the second-floor windows. This is very wrong in theory because it is bad construction to place a presumptive load above an opening, an area of glass. It is a very old principle that in good architecture, a member obviously calling for strength must *look* strong enough.

There is still a way out. It may be possible to add a wing, or an ell, if such features are not already there, and to make use of this as a real living room, the former one becoming (in traditional manner) the parlor. Figure 31 shows how some very discerning people solved their picture-window problem in just that way, while restoring a fine old home most intelligently. The original plan was the familiar one: a central hall, with rooms on each side, and an ell in the rear. The room on the first floor that is nearest to the camera is a big drawing room, with a handsome mantel between the windows, as the fenestration suggests. The room in the ell that is nearest to the main house is the dining room, chosen for its proximity to the kitchen and the charming view from what was then one small window. They widened that window as the picture shows, although it is partly hidden by the bush at the corner of the main house. The panes of glass in it are a trifle wider but the same height as those in the main house. To avoid too large a sash, they divided the window space with a narrow mullion, again helping to preserve the scale of the window. The kitchen lies behind the recessed porch at the right of the illustration. In front of this new dining room an outdoor dining space was arranged. Those who have had meals at both tables are sometimes a bit surprised that the view from indoors, through that window, is much more enjoyable than when seen from the outdoor table. It is more concentrated, agreeably framed by the window muntins. This was a modern alteration, made about 1946.

Many years before that, a shrewd Yankee trader named Simeon Colby settled in Dummerston Center. At that time this was a thriving community, the high plateau on which it stands being prosperous farming country. There he built a store, about 1791, and devised a clever idea for show windows that might offer a suggestion for a pair of picture windows for a dwelling which faced gable end to the street with an entrance in the middle. Figure 32 shows that it is "a natural" for a gable end. One may imagine a plan with the main entrance on the front, into a living room extending the entire width, a noble mantel and fireplace opposite the door. This would give a satisfactory composition.

Even if the experiment on fenestration was carried out only mentally, it may have demonstrated another architectural term, "scale." Making those small window rectangles of the experiment too large would make the house look tiny. If they had been cut unduly small, the effect would be that of a large, barrack-like building. The *scale*, in both cases, would be wrong.

"Scale," then, may be defined as the proportionate relationships of the elements of a building with some given standard. This is generally accepted as the height of a man. When Father builds a dollhouse for little Susie, he should scale it to the height of the doll for which it is built. One of the most tragic

32: OLD STORE, DUMMERSTON CENTER
North front; good fenestration

mistakes in all architectural history was made when St. Peter's at Rome was built to a gigantic scale unit. Anyone who visits it feels like a dwarf as he walks about in it. That may be good theology, but it is bad architecture. It has been said that "Michelangelo had the opportunity to erect the greatest cathedral in the world but only built the biggest."

Perhaps that seems a long way from discussing Early American farmhouses,

33: SARGENT-LEACH HOUSE, PAWLET
Front door and windows; note sash

but the principle is universal in application. Anyone who is restoring or enriching an old house should understand that a stock moulding which would be
exactly right as the crowning member of the exterior cornice would look
clumsy and "out of scale" on a living-room mantel. That the converse is true
was not always remembered by a few old-time housewrights. Proud of the
costly set of moulding planes, the usual gift to an apprentice when he had served
his time, one builder used them for the embellishment of *exterior* details, when
they had been intended for fine *interior* cabinet work. The unfortunate result
shows in Figure 40 over the little windows.

The scale of a house-front is set basically by its fenestration, and this is
influenced to a certain degree by the size and number of the small window

34: OLD BRICK HOUSE, HARMONYVILLE (TOWNSHEND)
East front; a study in fenestration

panes, especially if the muntins that hold them in the sash are painted white as they always should be. They keep the window openings from being merely black holes in the wall—the interior is always dark enough to give this effect, and white curtains cannot overcome it completely. The front door, too, seldom counts as strongly as the windows unless it is painted the same green as the blinds. The white sash and muntins, then, give a unity to the entire composition.

This is demonstrated by Figure 33 in a house that has the "front" on the long side and in Figure 34 by one which has its main face at the gable end. These two pictures should be considered together. The first not only has its original small-paned sashes (second floor) but later, Victorian, two-paned ones below. The other shows all three fashions; of the old, the middle, and the late periods. The twelve-pane sash was used until the 1840's, when the invention of new ways to make glass made it possible to buy larger panes. About that time the original sashes were replaced with new ones, each having but six panes. In the 1880's, similar advances in manufacturing brought still larger glass within pocketbook range. Figure 34 shows that only the lower sashes were replaced by the one-pane sort. The comparison of these shows better than many words the progressive deterioration in beauty and fitness. Fortunately, modern taste is more enlightened and fashion is swinging back again to the early period. Small-paned sashes are now available at most dealers in stock sizes.

Going back to the experiment for a moment, it must have been apparent when pairing the side windows that the middle window of the second floor and the door beneath it formed a focus for the front. This is more noticeable in Figure 33 than 34. The doorway of the first is unique in Vermont for beauty and ingenuity, although removing the blinds for the side lights would be an improvement.

A further, and last, experiment with the pieces of paper is to draw a thick pencil line around the door. This suggests that one of the "never-was-it" houses might be bettered by a very simple embellishment of the door casing, as shown in later illustrations. If the pencil lines are carried up to join the door with the window above it in some sort of a frame, it gives the idea that something really handsome could be developed on an otherwise plain house with a minimum of work, well within the ability of the average home craftsman. Moreover, if similar lines are drawn about the other window openings, it may suggest other apparently trivial, but really effective, improvements.

Usually the outside trim or "casings" of old windows is very plain, merely narrow boards of the same width at sides and top. The clapboards stop against the side pieces, or "stiles," to which the hinges of blinds or shutters are fastened. The top piece or "lintel" is usually capped by a narrow board, projecting a little in front and usually "flashed" with metal to throw out the water that runs down the walls. Only a very slight bit of work is needed to add a narrow moulding or "backband" around the three sides of the casings, perhaps replacing the top board with a wider one so the drip may fall farther out, and stopping the mouldings on the window sill. This makes something like a picture frame, and is shown in Figure 21 and also in Figure 35, even though the open blinds partly

35: BENEDICT-YOUNG HOUSE, WEST ARLINGTON
Window trim with backband

conceal the added richness of effect of the latter. Incidentally, that figure also shows a very bad example of gable-and-corner treatment. It is of a scale fitted to a much larger house and its clumsiness is apparent.

Some of the old houses of the early 1800's made the head casing wider than normal and used it as a frieze, adding a cornice to enrich the cap. This may be further developed, as shown in Figure 36, by using a dentil course in the miniature entablature. The frieze has odd little ornaments made of groups of five round rods (which might be dowel stock) flattened at the back and apparently nailed in place. A modern workman would doubtless reinforce this with marine glue, and painting would protect it. Merely projecting the board that forms the top of the window casing can do a good deal to dress up a housefront, as shown in Figures 30 and 33, but in Figure 37 this device is carried still further by making everything project more from the wall, so the mouldings of the side casings and the small entablatures cast richer shadows. These windows are in harmony with the really handsome entrance feature, in which the second-story window over the front door is made quite different from the flanking ones.

This doorway is a fine one, of the type that was frequently used in the Federal period, although the door itself is apparently of late Victorian design. The window above it is an arched one, repeating the design of the headlight of the doorway below. In its upper sash the small panes may be the original ones. The six-pane sashes of the lower half probably date from the time when all the other sashes were changed to their present design. In one respect this house may be a warning to modern house owners, for it is one of the very few buildings illustrated where blinds are a detriment to the design.

The terms "blinds" and "shutters" are almost universally confused. Both are framed like a small door, with top and bottom "rails" and side stiles and an intermediate rail set so the top panel is about half the height of the lower one. If these spaces are filled with slats, it is a blind. The slats, which are set at an angle, not only permit a person in the room to look *out* at a downward angle (for a somewhat limited view) but prevent an outsider from looking *in*. He is made blind by the blind. As a rule they are used on the second or bedroom floor and, as the slanting slats keep out rain while letting air in, are especially useful for night ventilation (Fig. 35).

The shutter has solid panels where the blind has slats, although the top panel

36: SAMUEL STRONG HOUSE, VERGENNES
Window trim with ornate cap

often has a decorative opening in it, a star or a leaf shape, a crescent moon or an anchor. When a house has both blinds and shutters this pierced panel, which admits air as well as a certain amount of light, is used in the blinds also for the sake of uniformity. Shutters are used on the ground floor, and when a summer resident closes his house for the winter the shutters are closed and bolted on

37: COBB HOUSE, STRAFFORD
Door and window headlights

the inside. Only a determined intruder could break in. Shut. Shutter. Just as simple as that.

It is unfortunate that most people do not realize that blinds and shutters have a practical usefulness that is quite as great as their decorative value and go to considerable expense for which the only return is good looks. If insect screens are of the full-length type, of course the blinds cannot be closed. But, as the best ventilation is obtained by opening the upper sashes, screens may be limited in size and cover only that area, placing them on the parting strips of the window frame. This is done by setting thin "runs" on it, which fit into grooves in the screen frame which is held in place by a suitable stop. When the time comes to remove the screen, the stop is pried loose and the screen slid out. In this method the upper sashes may be opened for cool night air and if the weather is rainy the blinds may be closed, giving protection to the open window.

In hot weather, naturally the windows both upstairs and down will be opened at night to cool off the house. The tendency is to leave them open all day, but this is a mistake. If windows and blinds are *shut* in the early morning while the house is at its coolest, the indoor temperature will not rise perceptibly all day, if the house is properly insulated. Enough light will be admitted through the slats of the blinds for welcome shade, and the fireplaces can be counted on to give enough ventilation to keep the air fresh. It is this use of blinds which is apparently unknown to most people. Their decorative value, generally recognized, is secondary to the little used practical one. Unfortunately, in the belief that they are merely ornamental, some have committed the unpardonable crime of nailing sham blinds, sometimes of strange shapes, on the walls at the sides of the windows. It is one of the new ideas that prove bad taste did not vanish with the Victorian era.

Storm sashes are essential for winter occupancy of most Vermont houses. Weather stripping is necessary too, but cannot take the place of the insulating cushion of air between the window and the storm sash. Most ready-made ones are four-paned, but if the permanent windows have small panes it is well worth going to the expense of duplicating their division, as nearly as is practical, in the storm sashes. That will partly compensate for the removal of the blinds and shutters, those highly decorative spots of green on the white clapboarded walls. They must be removed, for wintry gales are apt to loosen the hold of the

alleged "holdfasts" that served in summertime and with the storm sash oc-
cupying the space into which they normally close, they would swing wildly and
destructively, and could not be refastened without using a ladder—even if it
could be done in time. The best way of securing storm sashes is to use the customary hardware, a pair of hooks secured to the head casing that receive special
eyes screwed to the outside of the storm sash. These permit the storm sash to
be swung out a little for night ventilation of the bedrooms, and there are various
devices that hold the sash at the desired angle and secure it tightly when closed.
Of course the sash should be properly fitted, neither too tight nor so loose that
the wind blows through. Above all, *be sure* that every window that has or may
have blinds, shutters, storm sashes, or screens, has its number and that each of
these fitments bears the little plate or number tack that agrees with that fastened
on the window. No two openings are the same in *any* house and the variations
in old ones are greater than when they were new. It is a costly and temperish
job to get the right article in the right window, otherwise. These number tacks
may be bought at any hardware store and are much better than the old way of
denting Roman numbers on the window frames, etc., with the end of a broad
screwdriver.

Changing the outside of the house from summer to winter dress is no fun,
but it pays. Reliable experts figure that storm sashes and storm doors on the
exposed sides of a house may save enough fuel to pay for themselves in a couple
of years.

Attics get little light from the windows at the gable ends and, if subdivided,
need dormers, windows in the roof. Really old gable-roofed houses seldom had
them. They were often used in gambrel-roofed ones, generally as later additions
to the building, as they suit that sort of roof admirably. Figure 15 shows them
on an old Arlington house built in 1779 by a physician who soon started a
medical school there, the first in Vermont. He may have added the dormers to
give better sleeping quarters to his pupils. Note that they are built in what is
considered the best way, with sloping flat roofs which are extensions of the low-
pitched upper slope of the gambrel roof. The same picture shows the gabled
wing added by the Canfield family when they took over the house and its farm
after the doctor moved away. This has *gabled* dormers which are perfectly har-

38: CANFIELD-EHRICH HOUSE, ARLINGTON
Typical Georgian door

monious with the entire design. The secret of this is that the scale of both sorts of dormers has been kept small, in excellent relation to the house and its wing. The fact remains that no sort of dormer window is truly appropriate to the main roof of a two-story gabled house of formal Colonial type. Yet, dormers on the gabled roof of a small, one-story building, if kept small in scale, are not unattractive.

Another type of dormer which has recently appeared in the real-estate developments that spawn quantities of low-cost housing is a shed-roofed affair almost as long as the main roof, its front in the plane of the house-front, pierced by several windows. It is a cheap way to get more sleeping space in a small house but is certainly to be avoided as an alteration to a good house. Better add a wing or an ell than ruin a lovely building.

The front door, the main entrance, the entrance feature—a series of increasingly bombastic names—could greatly improve an unpretentious dwelling, lifting it from the commonplace to a modest degree of distinction. Probably that was one of the things that an apprentice learned from his master builder. Any amateur possessing good taste and handy with tools could take an idea from the examples shown here and develop it through a wide variety of designs.

Basically, the Georgian entrance was a paneled door surmounted by a headlight, needed to give some light to the stair hall. Usually the headlight was a semicircular sash with wooden muntins or lead "cames" in a variety of charming patterns. The casing often showed its family descent from stone features, being arched, with a keystone, all of wood (Figure 38). (A keystone is essential to a stone arch; in a wooden casing it is merely an ornament, and a meaningless one.) This arched doorway was flanked by pilasters, plain or fluted, with capitals, and carried short lengths of entablature surmounted by a "broken" pediment or gable, the word "broken" referring to the gap which gave room for the arched headlight. Details were at least reminiscent of the Classical orders, and despite their variations, the result was charming. The desirability of a closer relationship between such a door and the second-floor window above it is evident. At first, this window was given a round head in which the headlight design of the door was repeated in its upper sash, leaving the lower one to match its fellows, as in Figure 37.

39: EMERSON-DOUGLAS HOUSE, NORWICH
Door head and side lights

Little is known about the architects or master builders of early Vermont. Reference was made in the first chapter to Lavius Fillmore of Bennington, a well-trained young man whose sense of proportion and scale was notable. Another, Joseph Emerson, is known for his many dwellings built in the southerly part of Windsor County. By 1812 he had built up a large practise and reputation in that neighborhood. He built a fine house in Norwich for his parents in which he made a bold experiment in designing its entrance feature (Fig. 39). Instead of the conventional pilasters, flanking the doorway, he used a pair of wide panels, each containing a window filled with gracefully leaded glass. Above this is a surprisingly small-scaled broken pediment, its frieze (part capping one pier or panel, part the other) bearing a small and reticulated pattern. Only the main pediment has the customary corona. Its bed mould, repeated just above the frieze, consists chiefly of a row of tiny dentils which would be considered of very small scale even in a piece of cabinet work. This entablature is repeated on a larger scale, but still too small for its position, as the main entablature of the house! In that, however, the frieze pattern is a simpler network. Over this peculiar doorway he placed an arched window, dropping the sill as far as he could, in order to get the whole design in the available space. Even so, the arched window casing cuts into the main entablature. Some later owner, perhaps, had the bright idea of using blinds to give the effect of a Palladian window when they were open. While the composition has undoubted charm, it teaches the salutary lesson that famous housewrights of the past could, and did, make mistakes—and got away with them. However, this doorway has good ideas for the modern owner seeking inspiration.

If legend and architectural-detective findings are correct, and they seem to agree at any rate, the house near Bethel known as McKinstry Manor is also one of Emerson's products (Fig. 40). In the otherwise admirable entrance feature there is the same curious lack of proper scale in details noted in the Norwich house, a warning to modern craftsmen. The departures from the conventional design are successful, the work of one who is *almost* a master of his craft, as well as technically a master builder. The familiar Georgian doorway with arched headlight and broken pediment has an unusual treatment of pilasters used in this position. They have a little moulding running up the sides and returning, picture-frame-like, just above the normal base and beneath the cap of each.

40: MCKINSTRY MANOR, BETHEL

Scale of details too small

41: ROBINSON HOUSE, SOUTH READING
"New" main entrance

The "fair mansion" that Emerson built for Ebenezer Robinson was of much later date than the other two. The same errors of scale persist, but Emerson's style had changed with the times, keeping up with competitors in the area throughout which he worked. It is interesting to compare the view of the "new" Robinson House (Fig. 8) with the detail (Fig. 41). The semicircular headlight has been changed (by fashion's decree) to a graceful oval. The entablature gives a strong horizontal line, harmonizing with that of the eaves, and is supported on four pilasters which recall those of the McKinstry Manor door in their panelled shafts. Emerson stubbornly clung to his miniature-scaled mouldings and tiny dentils in the bed mould of the entablature and under the sills of the side lights. Years of weathering make them visible only by close inspection at the building.

By the end of the first third of the nineteenth century the cost of building with hired help seems to have affected fashion, and the arched-headlight type of entrance was replaced by doors with rectangular headlights, and, happily for the dwellers who had formerly stumbled about in dim halls, the addition of side windows flanking the front door, usually as a part of an entrance composition. A fine example of this type is in West Shaftsbury (Fig. 42). The house is a plain one, save for this noble entrance, designed by an unknown housewright of great ability. It is clear from the illustration that the hall into which this door opens is a very wide one, and the broad composition of the entire feature creates its serenity. The four pilasters are fluted and seem to be continued in the entablature above them, its lower portion breaking around each in a projection so slight that the cornice is not affected. The detail of the design is highly original in the employment of *two* rows of dentils, the larger one as the bed mould of the cornice. The present owner sawed the door apart so its upper half might be left open for air on hot days without danger of stray animals wandering into the coolness of the house, and added its row of dentils, an ingenious and pleasing accent. It would be an admirable doorway to copy—but beware of changing its proportions, or the scale of its parts! It is one of those designs that are easy to make but do not take kindly to alteration.

Another unknown genius, who probably had never seen the above entrance, designed one strikingly like it, skilfully and successfully altering its proportions and details. This, also, is a masterpiece (Fig. 43). Note the sturdy end pilasters

42: PERKINS-WHITE HOUSE, WEST SHAFTSBURY
Main entrance

43: DR. QUINN HOUSE, CASTLETON
Main entrance

44: ARNOLD-WEBB HOUSE, EAST ARLINGTON
Front door with side lights

and the more slender ones that flank the door itself, framing the side lights with their graceful leaded glass. The house itself is one of the most lovely in Castleton and one of the few handsome buildings in that quiet village that was not designed by its famous citizen, Thomas R. Dake. It is noteworthy for its tall columns (by no means a Southern monoply!) which carry the main entablature of the house, the sheltered front wall behind them ceiled with smooth matched boards, mostly very wide. These make a pleasing contrast with the narrow clapboards that cover the other walls of the house. Each of the four columns is turned from a single log, as may be seen from the seasoning check in one of them. The bases and capitals were turned integrally with the shaft. What a job! Nowadays, such columns are built up of thick locked and glued staves, something like a tall, slender barrel, and the caps and bases are not part of the shaft. The house was built about 1833 for Judge Clarke, evidently a quietly prosperous man. This entrance may be more useful as an inspiration to a modern workman than the preceding one because it would fit a narrower hallway, and one at the side instead of the middle of the façade.

A much plainer house of this type is shown in Figure 44; the ultimate simplification of the scheme, quietly charming, good in scale and proportions. For that reason it may be even more suggestive to a modern builder or restorer. There is no nonsense about it; plain flat door-trim with a backband, simple little side lights which range with the adjacent window in trim and glass height. Above the unadorned board frieze is a wide shelf-like affair with moulded edge and small bed mould to stiffen it. As an entrance feature, it bids the visitor welcome even if it offers little protection from rain.

The builders of very small houses, like that shown in the previous illustration, did not always go to the expense of headlight or side lights. The occupants apparently were not bothered by a dark hall, its only illumination borrowed from the second floor, or the windows of the adjoining rooms. Their descendants are not so easily satisfied, and many beautiful examples have been discarded in favor of a stodgy modern door, the upper half of which is one big pane of glass. It could be made much more sightly and still be practical if the space were filled with small panes resembling those of the adjacent windows.

Many of the plainer houses did a little to mark the importance of the front door. After all, even if the family always went around to the kitchen entrance

45: HOUSE AT BRIDGE, ARLINGTON
A simple doorway

46: OLD STORE, DUMMERSTON CENTER
Front door ; unusual trim

(as intimate friends did, too) the seldom-used main entrance was the important one, used for weddings and funerals, and, what probably was not realized by the occupants, formed a very important focus to the house design.

The doorways themselves, however simple, are well worth study and copying. The variety is very great. The example shown in Figure 45 is about as easy to construct as the preceding one. The plain, straightforward pilasters support an entablature that is only a little more elaborate, and the resulting composition enriches the little house without being over elaborate. The mouldings are so simple that satisfactory ones could be bought at any mill, if their size and scale are right.

Figure 32 shows an old country store, with admirable and very unusual fenestration. The main entrance (Fig. 46) has never been altered. Its stark simplicity no doubt pleased the shrewd and hard-boiled storekeeper. It is a very masculine design and is not only the focus of the front, but of sufficient vigor so that without it, the "Old Store" would have been utterly commonplace. It is a great contrast to the two doorways preceding, but it is emphatic without being pretentious. The store's original owner, Simeon Colby, may have been like that. With a few exceptions, doorways that were not the main or front entrance, were not ornamented in any fashion. Some of the old taverns, however, have quite elaborate side entrances, presumably for ladies, as they avoided the barroom.

Many old houses that stood alongside highways over which there was a good deal of traffic were the progenitors of modern Vermont's skiers' and tourists' lodging places. If the owners developed a flair for hotel keeping they might develop it to a tavern or inn. Obviously, the guests were to be made comfortable from the time of their arrival and a suitable welcome was important. From such feelings the porch, a desirable shelter for the main entrance from the vagaries of Vermont weather, became a feature of some old houses. One of these, illustrated in the Frontispiece, was on Governor Galusha's Shaftsbury home. Another, rather more elaborate, still stands in the northern part of the state on the Rich Tavern (Fig. 47).

Samuel Rich came up from Sutton, Massachusetts, in 1798 and pioneered seven hundred acres of land close to the present village of North Montpelier. Rich Hollow, as it was called then, was a thriving little settlement. It had water power that served a saw mill. A grist mill, a woolen mill, and even a distillery were included in the early industries from which he became prosperous. The woolen mill is still running, with an attractive showroom where tourists may buy good Vermont woolens, much more useful than the usual gifte shoppe souvenirs. He was soon joined by other settlers, for the hilly country had plenty of fertile farmland, not too rocky.

In 1805 he built a large tavern in a strategic location at the top of the hill south of the village, complete with barroom, a ballroom that occupied the entire front of the building on the second floor, and accommodations for the travelers on what was then a busy highway. It has a roomy, notably handsome covered porch, its front not unlike the fine Palladian window above it, with seats where post-prandial pipes could be enjoyed. It still offers its silent welcome, although the barroom which opens from it is "dry as a bone" today. Years ago the small-

47: RICH TAVERN, EAST MONTPELIER
Entrance front and covered porch

paned sashes were replaced by less pleasing ones. The big ballroom has been divided into bedrooms, and now that it is a farmhouse, some of its former glory has departed. Many of the attractive old details remain, however, some of which are illustrated in this book. These may provide suggestive and useful material for beautifying today's homes.

Pictures of authentic old work are always useful in making changes, but illustrations of modern alterations that have been well done can be equally helpful. An example of this is a recent improvement to the Mallory-Jones House in Castleton. The famous Thomas Dake designed this fine house for Lawyer Mallory about 1812. Half a century later its main entrance was all but hidden by a Victorian "Gothick" piazza. The present owner, with the aid of a skilful neighbor, demolished this and replaced it with the porch shown in Figure

48, using materials salvaged from the wreckage which were of good solid pine. The design is curious and unconventional, yet strangely in harmony with the rest of the house. If Dake's ghost ever walks the streets of his old home, Castleton, he would certainly approve of this new work. It is good to know that two persons who make no claim to architectural lore could evolve such an ingenious and successful result. Perhaps his ghost *did* walk, and guided them in their project.

Porches with roofs that give shelter from rain and downfalls of snow but have open sides without protection from biting winter winds should suggest adding a vestibule if the front hall is large enough for such a useful feature. Even with modern heating and good weather stripping, such a simple addition to the house plan might pay for itself in a short time. It is probably true that a vestibule will save a ton of coal a year, or its equivalent in oil. A housewright who worked in the neighborhood of Thetford devised a *closed* porch, something like an exterior vestibule, and persuaded several of his clients to adopt his new idea (Fig. 49). This has practical virtues, even if one criticizes details of the design, like the meaningless, windowless arched head and the flanking blinds made of slats of thin wood. The scheme never met with much approval, but the idea is a good one.

A variant of the covered porch forms the entrance to Lieutenant Governor Carpenter's house in Guilford (Fig. 50). It was built by a master builder who erected several other important dwellings in Windham County and his designs often included unconventional Palladian windows with *square*-topped middle elements as shown in this one, a piquant variant that has the advantage of being easy to make. The porch, with its effect of airy lightness, makes a very attractive and original entrance feature. He has also included in this building the first "piazza" in Vermont and it is even acceptable to the architectural purist who shudders at the later Victorian ones. It is in perfect harmony with the style of the house, partly from its location across the end wall, partly from the way its roof is supported by unadorned square posts with graceful arches between them. This motif appears later in the "continuous architecture" of some lengthy ells (Fig. 16), where instead of a projecting piazza there was a series of arched open bays used for farm equipment, two of them having a recessed porch behind the arches.

48: MALLORY-JONES HOUSE, CASTLETON
Entrance porch

49: FOWLE HOUSE, THETFORD
Enclosed entrance porch

50: BENJAMIN CARPENTER HOUSE, GUILFORD
"Palladian" window, porch, and piazza

These recessed porches, usually in ells, came into use in many parts of the state. Generally they were formed by moving an outer wall back into the kitchen or some other workroom, the roof being supported by a series of plain square posts on the line of what would have been the exterior wall of the ell. They were useful and good looking. If the ell were part of an inn and used for barroom or dining room, the recessed porch was a popular "sitting place" where the traveler might enjoy his after-dinner smoke more than on the crowded front porch. If this part of the building had two stories, the upper one was treated like the lower, doubling the area, as in Newfane Inn (Fig. 51).

The quiet little village of Newfane began its existence high up on "the Hill," for early settlers mistrusted the narrow river valley, with its seasonal floods and marshes formed by the numerous beaver dams. One of them, Jonathan Park, took a chance and cleared his land down in the fertile, level land where he built a saw and grist mill. A bit scornfully, the others called it "Park's Flats," but

51: THE NEWFANE INN, NEWFANE
Two-story recessed porches

when he had prospered and offered to give them free land from his large holding, the village literally "moved down," little houses towed by oxen and held back on the steepest part by the same powerful beasts. The inn was sawed in two, according to legend, its parts joined after they had reached the present site. There it stands today, a popular stopping place famed for its good food. The double-decked recessed porch is part of the original structure, its sturdy square posts, rounded to more slender columns in their upper half, supporting the roof. The curious and attractive reticulated railing is thought to be original, also, but the jigsawed brackets of the lower story probably replaced arched openings a mere century ago, and the shed-roofed piazza at the left of the picture is a later addition.

A country store without a gathering place for the menfolk is contrary to all tradition. It was a sure sign of summer when the Crackerbarrel Club moved out from behind the stove. The modern supermarkets have changed that part of village life, and not for the better perhaps. Garish signs, red-painted fronts and the like can hardly be called improvements. It is fortunate that a few of the old stores remain. Possibly when the Barrett family of Grafton erected the brick store (Fig. 52) across the road from their homestead it was not only a novelty in the village, it may have set a fashion. Better transportation reduced the need for large storage space for goods, as supplies could be brought in more easily, so the second floor could be used for office space. This was fortunate for the lawyer who was a member of the family. He was supplied with the necessary office space which was approached by a doorway at the end of the porch and his private staircase.

The brick building was erected in the 1840's and is not especially interesting except for its front porch, which is pleasing in its sturdy simplicity. The wooden pillars are neatly paneled, have well proportioned capitals and bases, and support a low pitched shed roof. The entire design is much better than in most buildings of that sort.

The majority of old houses did not have any sort of protection for the front door. Porches were the exception, not the rule. It is obvious from a study of the physical depreciation of dwellings that have not been kept in first-rate repair that the porch (where one existed) was the first part of the building to become decrepit. This may explain why so large a majority of dwellings never had one; it was considered a luxury, something unnecessary. Yet there were a few master builders who felt differently. One of them—or perhaps two or three innovators existed—devised an inexpensive and at the same time a *durable* means of giving protection to the visitor waiting at the door, by recessing the entrance, pushing it back into the hall where, usually, there was plenty of unused space.

A house in East Dorset is one of the earliest examples of this new fashion (Fig. 53). Later on, some occupant enamored of Victorian fashions effectively concealed it by one of the deplorable piazzas that are being demolished in these days. When the present owner brought it in sight again the entire appearance of the house was changed, for it is a very plain building and the door is notably impressive. The maligned Victorian piazza can be given some praise, however, for it preserved the narrow claphoards of the original house from the decay that made replacement necessary on the second-story level. Granting that the

52: BARRETT STORE, GRAFTON
Street front and piazza

53: BEEBE-HOYT HOUSE, DORSET
Recessed front door

54: SIDNEY CROFUT HOUSE, WEST ARLINGTON
Recessed front door with columns

55: MCCABE HOUSE, WEST ARLINGTON
Recessed front door, variant

out-of-scale corner blocks are not very pleasing, the lovely tracery of the headlight and side lights form a charming decoration, worthy of imitation.

Most of these recessed doorways are of later date. Samuel Buck, who built scores of houses in the vicinity of Arlington during the 1850's, used this recessed-entrance scheme in many of them, ringing the changes on its details so no two of his buildings are quite alike, save, alas, in one feature: he seems to have been quite unable to design a really good upper member of an entablature.

Figure 54 is a picture of the main entrance of his own home. The corner blocks of the "frame" of the recess are reminiscent of those shown in the preceding figure, much better scaled, but lacking imagination. The slim columns are unconventional, but the idea is an excellent one. Unfortunately, the crowning entablature or cornice is made up of a series of square-edged boards, without any mouldings. Despite these criticisms, the underlying *idea* of the design is so good that one longs for a modern craftsman with good taste to use it as the starting point of an entrance feature that could be made a brilliant success. It is worth remembering that a great deal may be learned by studying mistakes, especially, perhaps, if they have been made by other persons.

Another of Buck's recessed doorways is the main entrance of his largest and handsomest house. It stands almost directly across the little river from his own home, an impressive building that he attached to a small but lovely one, now the east wing of the composition. This doorway (Fig. 55) is well proportioned in mass, but illy developed in its details. The simple, pleasing pilasters are just right. The architrave of the entablature they support is not. Its mass is good, but the monotonous steps of the square-edged boards that compose it grieve the judicious. The frieze is plain, as it should be, but too narrow and, again, the cornice is sadly unimaginative in detail, mass, and scale. This, too, is a fine idea that should challenge a home craftsman. Little changes of little things would make the composition a notable one. The two pictures, then, might do more to help a person who is about to restore an old house than other, excellent, examples that have been shown.

Improvements to doorways like those illustrated and described in the previous paragraphs can easily be made with a minimum of labor and expense.

There are other cases, those where a fine doorway has been removed, either sold to someone who was willing to pay an attractive price or torn down, the victim of neglect or of our New England winters. Sometimes plain boards have been set to cover the casing against the weather. They are unlovely. Home owners who have the desire to restore ancient beauty and are able to pay the slight cost of restoration could not be content with such a scar. The class of houses termed "never-was-its" previously, also shows drab and uninteresting treatment of the doorway in many cases.

Whatever the cause of the deficiency, it can and should be rectified. The quiet charm of a well-proportioned, well-kept home deserves a fitting entrance, harmonizing the exterior and the interior, extending a welcome to friends and guests. "Come in, come in; warm your body and your heart!" should be its message.

[V]

STAIRWAYS

—◆•◆•◆—

THE STAIRCASE is the largest single element of decorative construction inside a house, as well as the most important functional one. It is much more than just a means of getting to the next floor. Many an ancient dwelling, plain as a pikestaff on the outside, has a quiet beauty of interior details that goes with gracious living. A stranger, appreciating the hospitable charm of the entrance door, is greeted by a revealing glimpse of hall and stairway that gives a suggestion of the family surroundings. It is an introduction to the rooms where they live, even if the very fact of the rising stairs suggests that the next floor is a private region.

The old builders realized these characteristics when they designed their stairs. It must be acknowledged that the comfort of those using them seems to have been of little concern to the long-legged pioneers, but they did make an effort to make stairways decorative, from the earliest days of Vermont house building. As time passed and people became wealthier they devised an astonishing variety of plans and ornamentation for the staircase.

Before discussing stair design in detail it may be desirable to describe the usual construction and to define some technical terms. If the owner of an old house desires to make changes in its stairs he will certainly need skilled help and he can get on better with his workmen if he is familiar with their terminology.

A properly built staircase consists of steps supported by carriage beams, often called "strings." The horizontal part of the step is called, understandably, the "tread" and the adjoining vertical portion is the "riser." The lengthways joints between tread and riser are akin to the familiar "tongue and groove" of floorboards. A tread has a tongue at the back, formed from part of its surface, which fits into a groove on the bottom of the riser above it. The front part of the tread is rounded, and overhangs the riser next below it by about 1 1/4 inches. This overhang is called the "nosing" and usually has a small moulding beneath it, largely for decoration. Behind this small moulding is the front surface of the riser of the next step below. This has a tongue on it, fitting into the lengthways groove cut in the bottom surface of the tread, which is made of hardwood and about 1 1/8 inches thick for strength. The risers are usually of softwood and customarily 3/4 of an inch in thickness, so there is ample material in which to cut the tongues and grooves. The total assembly of a step is, then, L-shaped.

The carriage beam or "wall string" is firmly spiked to the studs of the hall partition at the requisite angle (of which more will be said later). An L-shaped groove or "housing" is cut about 3/4 of an inch deep in the wall string, to receive the end of the step. The upper surface of this groove which receives the end of the tread is cut accurately to the horizontal. The front or outer surface of the groove or housing which is to receive the riser is, of course, cut at right angles, accurately. The *lower* surface of the horizontal housing recess and the *inner* surface of its vertical part are *not* cut parallel to the exposed surface of tread and riser, but at a slight angle. When the assembled step is placed in the housing recess, wedges of hardwood are driven tightly in the spaces between housing recess and bottom of the tread and the back of the riser, wedging them firmly in place. They are usually kept there by good glue. If, after a century or so, shrinkage or failure of the glue loosens the step in the housing, a squeak results when a weight comes on it. If the under side of the stairway is exposed, this may be stopped by driving the loosened wedge in tighter.

The assembly of the outer part of the stairs may differ considerably from the above. If, however, the outer string is made of dressed lumber with the intention of exposing it to view when finished, the process is the same as for the wall-string except that the outer string may be carried by a stud partition immediately beneath it. The string, therefore, conceals the step-ends as shown in Figure 56. This is a "closed string" staircase, a type that is found only in very old houses. It is occasionally used for a straight run, but more often is found in a

56: GRAVES HOUSE, SHAFTSBURY
Closed string stairway

57: KNIGHT PLACE,
DUMMERSTON CENTER
Closed string stairs, richer detail

very small house with a central chimney where a winding stair is necessary. These will be described later. In the picture both the wall string and the outer one are shown. The outer string may have an additional, strengthening, timber set under it to receive the studding of the little triangular wall which fills the space between string and floor. The design shown here is severely plain. Everything is square: the newel, the hand rail, and the spindles between rail and string. The one touch of ornament is the thin piece of wood that caps the newel. Even this is functional, since it covers the end grain of the newel. The moulded edge of the rail (Fig. 56) gives a better grip for the hands which may clasp it for support. That may have been needed! The house was built as an inn, either a trifle before 1800 or soon after. Guests who had imbibed buttered rum on winter nights may have been glad of a sturdy timber to grasp on their way to bed.

Another stairway of this type is in the Knight Place, in Dummerston Center (Fig. 57). Originally this building was a tavern, erected in 1794 by Simeon

Colby, whose store and its doorway are shown in the previous chapter. The pleasing balustrade indicates that Colby had a liking for more ornamental elements of a building than were to be found in the neighborhood. It is also a closed-string staircase and leads up to a large wainscotted hall from which one enters the ballroom. The construction is the same as in the other example, but much more decorative. The wainscot on the wall side, of plain but wide boards with a little cap moulding, the mouldings that outline the outside string, and those of the hand rail, the well-designed cap of the newel, but above all, the lathe-turned balusters, even to the little half-baluster that is set against the inner face of the newel post, show what results may be obtained when an owner who cares teams up with a workman who knows his craft.

The other type of staircase is the "open string," the familiar sort that is practically universal nowadays. It differs from the closed string variety in the way the outer ends of the treads and risers are supported. Instead of being "housed" into the outer string (as they still are to the inner one), this outer string has step-size notches. The tread rests on the flat part of the notch, its end projecting out beyond the string with a nosing, like that on its front edge. The riser is set flat against the vertical part of the notch, and its end is flush with the outer face of the string. The outer string is firmly secured to the newel post at the bottom and to the framing beams of the house at the top of the opening called the "stairwell" (Fig. 58). Usually, there is a stiffening beam (or two of them if the stairs are wide) set between the strings to support the junctions of tread and riser. Often this is not notched. These are called "carriage beams" and are usually concealed. They provide a surface on which lath may be set if the under side of the staircase is plastered—effectively preventing tightening the wedges to stop squeaks!

The open string poses a problem for the stair builder, for the end wood of both tread and riser is exposed and end grain is unsightly and hard to conceal with paint. It is still more difficult if the wood is to be finished natural, with stain and varnish. There are two ways to overcome this. A practical solution to this problem is to miter the joint between the riser and the outside string. This is a time-consuming operation and, while most effective in concealing the end grain of the riser, lacks the compensation of being decorative also. The

58: ROBINSON HOUSE, SOUTH READING
Hall and stairs in new addition

59: SARGENT-LEACH HOUSE, PAWLET
Open string stairs, twin newels

easier solution is to cover it with a piece of wood so thin that its end grain is almost invisible, ornamentally jigsawed, as shown in the upper part of Figure 58. This will be discussed later and appears in many of the illustrations.

While the steps are of course the principal part of a staircase, they are almost entirely functional. On the other hand, the balustrade consisting of newel, rail, and balusters, is functional in that it provides protection and safety to those who use the stairs, but decorative also, as it sets the tone of the interior of the dwelling. It may vary from extreme plainness to considerable elaboration. It must be strong, but need not be clumsy.

The newel is the sturdy post at the start of the stairs, and usually has a mate on the second floor, with intermediate ones if the run of the stairs changes direction in the ascent. It is always square in cross section at the bottom, so it may be very firmly secured to a framing timber, as well as at or near its top where the rail is fastened to it. In the earliest examples it was square throughout its entire height, the only ornament a little cap fastened on top which hid the end grain (Figs. 56, 57). In later years, with the changes that accompanied greater material prosperity, the square cross section was limited to the upper and lower parts of the post, and the space between was lathe turned (Fig. 58), adding decorative value. Strength seemed to be an obsession with some of the early housewrights, and in one old house, known for its fine ornament everywhere but in the staircase, there are *two* solid, plain square newels at the foot of the main staircase (Fig. 59), which is also furnished with an unusually massive handrail. The big house was built by a physician, who conducted one of Vermont's first medical schools in addition to his practise—he may have expected a lively set of students! Going to the other extreme, there are some very attractive examples of slender newels, retaining their square cross section from bottom to top but gently tapered. In these the newel termination is treated like a tenon and is set into the end of the rail, instead of the rail being secured to the newel (Fig. 60). It might be thought that such a design would develop some symptoms of weakness, as it looks fragile, but they seem perfectly firm today even if most of them have been in use nearly a century and a half. Durable hardwood and expert craftsmanship may be the explanation.

The rail, the top member of a balustrade, was made very plain at first, merely a rectangular stick of wood not unlike the modern two-by-four, with its upper surface rounded off, almost massive in appearance. Big hands could grasp it, but the smaller hands of women and children were better served by the later refinements of this feature, when it was made less bulky. Its bottom, as before, was kept flat so the balusters might be firmly secured to it, although the cross section was changed so the curved upper surface lapped over the sides. Occasionally the entire rail section was made oval, with a small flat on the bottom to receive the balusters. The illustrations show these various forms far better than can be explained in words.

In the earliest staircases the rail was straight throughout its length, its ends cut off at an appropriate angle to the vertical face of the newel in order to make a firm connection with it. All of this was within the abilities of a good carpenter,

60: STONE TAVERN, ALBURG
Noteworthy stair details

as it would be today for a home craftsman. There was a tendency, however, among the housewrights to develop new and more decorative things which could be better done by the skilled specialists, the stair builders. These men began to abandon straight rails, for example, using graceful curves called "easements" where the rail and newel joined (Fig. 61), which were especially useful if the newel was to fit, like a tenon, into a mortise cut in the under side of the end of the rail. They devised various ways of treating the exposed end of the rail, which had previously butted against the newel, even going so far as to widen it out to a circular cap, its edges of the same moulding as the rail itself, using this as the crowning feature of the lathe-turned newel (Fig. 62). In addition to this relatively simple form of easement, they developed the spiral where the balustrade reached the second floor and turned back to the horizontal run of the stairwell, thus eliminating the upper newels that formerly were repetitions of the one at the foot of the stairs. Some housewrights, anxious to keep up with the fashion but lacking the skill to construct even the curved easement

61: MISS HALL'S HOUSE, GRAFTON
Stair detail, rail with easement

62: H. W. CONGDON HOUSE, ARLINGTON
Newel, balustrade, step-ends

at the newel, made an angular joint in the rail to attain the desirable horizontal piece into which the newel might be set (Fig. 60), keeping to the newel of conventional form on the second floor.

The stair builders, however, were ingenious men with a realization of the importance of the start of a balustrade. Even a well-turned newel did not give quite the emphasis they felt was desirable. The only thing to do, they seem to have decided, was to use their skill in curving the rail like a snail shell with the newel as its core. That essential feature retained its necessary structural strength but was somewhat reduced in decorative importance, as it was inclosed in a cage of balusters (Fig. 63). Very wisely, these were kept plain, the conventional and efficient spindles with square cross sections. The entire structure was given a suitable base by extending the tread and riser of the bottom step with a round end similar to the curve of the rail. The newel, reduced in size but still sturdy, pierced the step and the under floor, and was securely attached to the framing

63: PARRISH HOUSE, RANDOLPH CENTER
Hall and stairs, balustrade

64: SIDNEY CROFUT HOUSE,
WEST ARLINGTON
Stair detail, turned balusters, newel

timbers. Sometimes it was rather plain in design, but as often it was lathe turned as in the illustration.

This scheme became very popular and was used from its beginning in the early 1800's until Victorian fashions superseded it. One of the latest is in the house Samuel Buck built for his own home about 1850 (Fig. 64). This shows the decadence in architectural quality which marks that period everywhere. As in so many other Colonial houses, the step proportion is not good, but the noticeable difference from the previous example is the lack of contrast in the design. The newel is a turned one, far from exciting, and the balusters are lathe turned in the same pattern but of smaller diameter.

Plain square-section balusters (spindles) are quite as common in stairs of the later years as in the earliest, and their popularity may be due to the definite effect of light on the flat surfaces of a square or rectangular cross section as compared with a turned one. Reference to the illustrations will show this (Figs. 56, 60, 62). Balusters, other than the turned ones, have a virtue that is not shared by the rail or newel; an amateur, a home craftsman, can easily replace broken ones and even substitute the better square- or rectangular-section ones for others that seem to be of less pleasing design. To be sure, if a handrail has no easement and is in poor condition or seems undesirable to keep for any other reason, it, too, may be replaced, using stock material from the lumberyard, for well-designed handrails can be bought. Plain balusters may be made in the home workshop, the square-sectioned ones sawed out from boards of appropriate thickness. The rectangular ones are a little harder to make, for while they may be cut from 5/8-inch wood, they should taper from bottom to top, starting 1 1/2 inches wide and diminishing to an inch at the top. They look best if the edges are rounded to a semicircle, which may be done with a shaper attachment for a drill press. The bottoms should be dovetailed into the tread, back of the piece of nosing that hides its end wood. The top can be toenailed into the rail with brads of suitable size. More elaborate work on stairs needs a professional stair builder, who will have his own shop and the necessary machinery to make easements, and perhaps even "snail-shell" spirals to cap the newels.

The foregoing pages have dealt chiefly with the parts of the staircase as found in existing old houses, their details, and possible restoration. The plan or shape of a staircase layout is largely determined by the plan of the house and is worthy of study. Occasionally a buyer finds a place that he likes, with a fine view and ample water supply, but the house may be undesirable or in poor repair. Perhaps its barn is of framed construction and in a better location than the house. The difference between the skeleton of a barn and a house is surprisingly small if the former is of the old-time construction described earlier in this book, and it may be made into a satisfactory dwelling even without the addition of an ell or a wing. In this case a study of the layout of the stairs that will be needed, in relation to the adaptations of the skeleton to a desirable house plan, can be very useful.

The earliest houses had a big central chimney with large fireplaces serving the rooms on three sides. The fourth side was a small entrance hall, its area insufficient for what we now call a safe and comfortable stairway. Instead, it was narrow, steep, and twisting as it wound its way upward. Old folks and children on their way to bed went laboriously up a few steps, built with high risers and narrow treads, to a small platform, often one with "winders," which

65: PARSON DEWEY HOUSE, OLD BENNINGTON
Steep old stairs without balusters

66: OLCUTT-JOHNSON HOUSE, NORWICH
A compact hall; the balusters help

67: BRADLEY HOUSE, WESTMINSTER
A wide hall and fine staircase

are diagonal steps, radiating from the newel as a center. Taking that sharp turn they climbed up a few more steps to another narrow platform, too often with winders also, and finally reached "the haven where they would be" (Fig. 65). No wonder an old Vermonter said, caustically, "'Twould be awful hard to get a coffin down them stairs with the corpse in it." In many cases the straight runs were so short that there was no room for balusters—merely a handrail between newels. Small children could not reach as high as the handrail for support. "Tumbling down stairs" was a frequent discomfort for them, and the joy of "sliding down the banisters" was for later generations. Fortunately, larger houses of this type could get room for balusters, plain but efficient (Fig. 66).

When the more typical Colonial plan was developed with its central hall

flanked by pairs of rooms, the stair builders had more latitude. Perhaps some
of them remembered painful bumps in their childhood. At any rate all the
houses of this plan in its earliest developments had stairs with *straight* runs,
like those in Figures 56 and 57, and the halls were sufficiently wide so the stairs
could be increased in width, safety, and comfort, even if the last was rather
uncommon. If the hall was quite wide (without being extravagantly so) there
might be a change of direction at the top of the staircase, a right-angled turn
without winders, which gave more room below between the first step and the
front door (Fig. 58). This made a wide space on the second floor between the
stair well, protected by its balustrade, and the front wall. If the house had
a big Palladian window in that location, the light was good and the quiet, retired
nook was an admirable place for the housewife to do her sewing or, in earlier
times, to set up her spinning wheel. In other cases, the stairs were kept well
towards the front, and the turn made more space for a small room at the back
of the house on the second floor. In the large houses the central hall was often
very wide, and the staircase made its change of direction after only a few steps
up (Fig. 67) so its handsome balustrade and the rich effect of the step-end
decorations which covered the end grain of the risers might be fully seen and
appreciated. In this instance the housewright lost no opportunity for suitable
decoration, but unfortunately he used winders with the narrow part of their
treads unavoidably at the critical point where the two handrails are far apart.

Safety as well as comfort in using a staircase depends on the proportion of
riser height to tread width. This is recognized by organizations that have a
financial interest in reducing accidents, like the Workmen's Compensation
Bureau, but disregarded by most house-building firms, just as it was by the old-
time housewrights, who apparently were not interested in step proportions.
The stairs in most old houses are excellent in appearance and sturdily built,
but their steps are seldom comfortable and sometimes really dangerous. This
is peculiar, for it is not true of those being built in England at the time our
Vermont craftsmen were borrowing decorative details from that country. It is
still harder to understand why wrongly proportioned steps are still being built
today. There seems to be a feeling among the planners of "developments" that

better stairs than those they provide are a "waste of room." The people who buy these houses accept uncomfortable stairs without realizing that they are also hazardous.

In many cases nothing can be done to better the stairway of an old house except at considerable expense. When building a new one or altering an old extensively, there is no excuse for using wrong step proportions. There are rules which, if followed intelligently, assure steps that are *safe* as well as comfortable. Their purpose is to minimize the hazard of stumbling and to provide stairs with proportions which will meet the needs of persons of "average" size. These rules can seldom be followed exactly, and minor adjustments may be necessary to meet special conditions. They are based on data tested by use and have a common starting point, a riser 6 inches high and a tread 12 inches wide, which is generally accepted as optimum. Rule "A" deals with permissible variations from this starting point and regulates them by limiting the product of the two dimensions, which must not be less than 72 nor exceed it much. Rule "B" takes the angle of slope of the staircase as the controlling factor, which is 26 degrees for a series of 6×12 steps but may be steeper, as much as 35 degrees, before the variations produce steps that are considered hazardous.

Fundamentally, both rules are derived from studies of the travel of the foot when ascending or descending a staircase. As the entire weight of the user is borne by the ball of first one foot, then the other, the shifting balance and the muscular effort of a theoretically *average* person determine the acceptable variations from a 6×12 step. It is obvious that these are very different for a tall and athletic man from what would suit a dainty Miss, and for both extremes in human size a compromise must be made in riser height and tread width. A combination of both rules would seem to be desirable in planning a new staircase or rebuilding an old one. The usual overhang of the tread due to the nosing helps considerably in determining the proper width of the tread which affects the sense of balance when going down stairs. It should never be necessary to descend crab fashion, the feet at an angle to the direction of travel, yet that is what a person with only an average length foot must do on cellar stairs with their usual pernicious and hazardous 8×8 dimensions. No wonder this is the place where most domestic accidents happen.

Stairways with 6×12 steps are about as rare as "average" men and women,

68: GOVERNOR GALUSHA HOUSE, SHAFTSBURY
Staircase detail

so variations from that desirable norm are almost universal. Steps in modern houses frequently have 7-inch risers and 10-inch treads which do not meet the "acceptable" rating by Rule "A," because the riser is too high for the comfort of many women and the tread perilously narrow for a tall man with long feet. Also, the product of the two dimensions is 70 instead of 72, and the slope angle is the steepest that is permissible under Rule "B." Widening the tread a mere half-inch would give a feeling of greater security to the man, although the woman would not be helped. Yet this is considered a notably "easy" stairway to use, compared with many old and new ones. Decreasing the height of the riser to 6 1/2 inches and keeping the 10 1/2-inch tread is a great improvement. And increasing the tread to 11 inches, making a 6 1/2 × 11 step, would provide a close approximation of the optimum under rule "A," 71 1/2, as well as "B," with a slope of 28 degrees. In all cases, the overhang of the nosing is what engineers call a "factor of safety." It is an addition to the nominal width.

Old houses show examples of all sorts of variations from the modern norm. Persons who fall heir to an old house with stairs that seem undesirable even in these tolerant days, should consult an ingenious and trustworthy carpenter but endeavor to keep close to the two rules lest the suggested remedy be worse than the disease.

Anyone planning a new house would do well to design the staircase first, the overall dimensions determining whether it is to be a straight run or to have a change of direction near the top. There must be ample head room above the tread that comes under the end of the stairwell, and 6 1/2 feet is a minimum. If there is a change of direction there should be a square flat landing between the two sets of steps, as "winders" or diagonal steps are generally hazardous at best. One winder might be used if its riser is moved away a few inches at the newel and then slanted towards the wall so its tread, about halfway of its length, may approximate the width of the others. If it is made in the usual way, with its riser starting at the newel, it will be shaped like a slice of pie, very wide at the far end and without usable width close to the newel, a dangerous hazard when descending the staircase. More than one winder on a platform invites trouble.

The advantage of planning the stairs first is that they may be designed with suitable proportions. All the risers must be of the same height, their sum equal to the floor-to-floor height, for a change of riser height is almost certain to cause

69: CANFIELD-EHRICH HOUSE, ARLINGTON
Staircase detail

a user to stumble. This also permits treads to be of the desired width and the stairwell to be suited to them. Many old stairways have badly proportioned steps because the floors were framed before the stairs were planned without considering desirable step proportions.

A good many old houses were built with severely plain staircases. These afford opportunities for enrichment at little cost, if the work is done by a local carpenter, or by the owner, if he is skilled with tools. Sometimes "improvements" in what we feel to be questionable taste were made during the Black Walnut era. Figure 5 is an example. It would not be difficult to remove that clumsy black-walnut newel and replace it with one suitable to the style of the rest of the house. Other stairways could be considerably improved in appearance if their ultra-plain outer strings could receive simple embellishment, like a moulding on the bottom edge (Fig. 61). At least the exposed end grain of their risers might be covered.

Care must be used with jigsawed cutouts on the riser ends that their material is not too thick. Some of our forebears were not sensitive to such refinements. Figure 68, for example, is a detail of the main stairway in Governor Galusha's house to which reference has been made previously. It is not only clumsy in appearance, but the inevitably exposed end grain of the thick cutouts, which is impossible to conceal, adds to the crudity of the effect. There is another, more easily corrected error shown in this staircase. The dark paint of the risers is a detriment to the composition. It would be better if risers, newel cap, and balusters were painted white.

Solid wood stock that is thin enough for cutouts can have the end grain of its edges sandpapered almost to invisibility. Today we use 1/8-inch plywood, made up of three layers, their grain crossing, and the end grain can scarcely be seen even if not sandpapered. In the Enos Canfield House (Fig. 69) the wood of the cutout ends is of slightly thinner stock than the governor's and their front ends are mitered into the risers, hiding the end grain. The vertical line of the back, echoing the front, is a very unusual feature, an experiment by Wilmot, a housewright from Massachusetts. People like it for its honesty and novelty. The handrail, too, is very good. Its curved top curls over the rectangular body of the rail in a manner that gives a comforting feeling of security to the user.

The spindles of the balustrade are square in section, set with their diagonals in line with the rail, enriching that simple form of construction, with half-spindles set against the newels at top and bottom of the flight, another suggestion worth copying.

Alburg, in the extreme northwest corner of Vermont, is an old town on the long tongue that extends down from Canada into the upper waters of Lake Champlain. Known for many years for its building stone and fine colored marbles, many of its better houses are built of stone from local quarries, and are extremely plain on the outside. The enrichment of their interiors with fine cabinet work of features like mantels was a natural outlet for the builders' love of beauty. The Old Stone Tavern, built in 1823, is one of these structures. It has a good staircase (Fig. 60) with interesting and unusual detail. The step-end cutouts are sawed in a graceful pattern and are unique in the addition of a carved "tear-drop" cut into the substance of the thin wood and clear through it, down to the surface of the string. The spindles are square in section. The newel is also square and tapers from its base to the slender top, which is sunk into the handrail. Treads, newel, and rail are made of cherry, aged to a lovely color. The end of the rail has an inlay, diamond shaped and made of white maple, a very unusual but pleasing decoration not too difficult for some home craftsman who wanted to "go and do likewise."

The preceding pages of this chapter, and its illustrations, have dealt with existing staircases and their details in old Vermont houses, but have made only a few references to what owners may do to improve their appearance. The three examples of old work shown and described above suggest that there is a great deal that can be done today for the houses classed as "never-was-its," buildings erected after the decline of the Colonial style. Their interiors may easily be improved in appearance by those who can use tools and do their own work. The stairs, perhaps, are uncomfortable, but "What can't be cured must be endured" as far as structural matters go. However, they certainly can be embellished to a degree that would be worth while. It has already been suggested in the previous pages that an unsuitable newel can be replaced with one that is more pleasing. It is also possible that the string, if drearily plain, can have various things done to it that are easy for a home craftsman, and may be the obvious place to make alterations. Closed-string stairs need no added embellish-

70: HOUGHTON HOUSE, ST. ALBANS
Staircase detail

ment, so that form may be passed over and the improvements in appearance of the open-string ones considered, taking the junction of risers with string first.

If the end grain of the risers is left exposed, even if it has been carefully sandpapered so paint almost conceals it, thin and narrow strips of wood may be bradded over the end of the risers, their surfaces flat, or reeded as shown in Figure 61. In that example, a moulding has also been added at the bottom of the string, and the total effect is all that might be desired. It would be very easy to do with stock materials if the thin strip is left flat. It could readily be reeded by an amateur who had a drill press with a shaper attachment and a variety of knives, such as may be obtained from one of the mail-order houses. Or, two plain strips might be used, clasping the corner of the riser in an L-shape, as shown in Figure 62. If the jigsawed step-ends are wanted, there is a wide variety of patterns in the previous illustrations, but only that in Figure

71: DAKE HOMESTEAD, CASTLETON
Staircase detail

62, a modern example, is made of 1/8-inch plywood. The others vary from 1/2 inch to thicker and hence less desirable ones.

A good many old stairways, especially in the later periods, were constructed with a miter joint between riser and string so there was no necessity for covering that joint. However, the old housewrights felt the step-end was a good place for some sort of decoration that did not imply a practical use and nailed mouldings to the string, usually forming a quadrangle that echoed the adjoining lines, horizontal, vertical, and sloping (Fig. 70). These, with the addition of similar mouldings on the lower part of the string, did a good deal to make a stairway with a simple balustrade more ornamental. There are other examples of this sort of embellishment in the illustrations of this chapter.

The carved ivy vine on the staircase string in the Soule House in Fairfield (Fig. 5) is unique in its way, for it is carved in relief, by cutting away all the blank surface of the string, an expense that seems incredible today. That famous

Castleton architect, Thomas Reynolds Dake, designed and carved the spirally curving string of the stairs in his own home, making a differently unique embellishment. One is carved in relief, the other, Dake's, incised (Fig. 71). It is a simple but ingenious pattern, done entirely with one tool, a keen wood carver's gouge. Perhaps it should not be included in this book, which does not show any of Vermont's very beautiful spiral staircases, of which this is one of the simplest. It is just barely possible that some wood-carving enthusiast might use the picture as a hint of quite a different way of using his skill to adorn a plain string. For Dake, it was a labor of love. It was the main staircase of the house he built for his bride according to old-time custom. He was young and talented, but as this was one of the first houses he built—and he built many— it is interesting to see that he had not yet learned that the end grain of risers should not be exposed to view. A century and a half of painting and repainting has not concealed a young man's error. If he ever repeated it, one of the many fires in the village has removed that lapse from good craftsmanship.

We admire the works of men like Dake but need not be blind to their mistakes nor repeat them in the dwellings we build. As far as it is practical we should endeavor to rectify them in old houses, especially by eliminating errors that create hazards to the family. Steep cellar stairs can at least be made safer if provided with a handrail. Even a schoolboy could make that essential improvement. Replacing a badly designed main staircase is a job for the professional, difficult and costly, but an amateur craftsman with home workshop power tools can change the appearance of a commonplace entrance hall and its stairs into something distinguished. That would be well worth the time and effort.

[VI]

INTERIOR FEATURES

————◆•◉•◆————

A STAIRWAY is functional in character, but, as has been shown, it may be a valuable part of any well-considered scheme of interior decoration. The mantel, as the focus of an important room and therefore affecting its architectural worth, like stairways, needs a chapter to itself. In between are the lesser decorative features of which this chapter treats. The door and window trim, too often considered as trivia, should be something better looking than plain flat boards that cover the gap between frames and plaster. If this fact was not realized when the house was built, the new owner may easily rectify the mistake. Some treatment of the lower wall, even if it is only a chair rail, can do much to unify a room. The various kinds of wainscot may lift a commonplace room from mediocrity.

A room is best judged when it is completely empty, free of the distractions of rugs, furniture, and draperies. True, they can banish barrenness if they are well chosen, but why be content with a barren room when it can be so easily improved? If such improvements are added, the "rugs, furniture, and draperies" will have an even better chance to contribute to the desired effect.

"Plain trim" of a door or window consists merely of three flat boards a few inches wide. The top one (head casing) is set flat on the side ones, its two ends showing end grain. This may have been sandpapered smooth but often this has not been done. If the opening is a window, these side casings rest on the window sill, below which is its apron, everything square-edged. If it is a door, the side casings of course rest on the floor and the baseboard stops against them. Very plain; too plain.

72: H. W. CONGDON HOUSE, ARLINGTON
Plain backband trim

The cure is a simple one, easily done by an amateur carpenter in various ways, often a little at a time. The easiest is to add a "backband" (Fig. 72), which is a stock moulding to be bought at any lumberyard or mill. It is about 1/4 inch thicker than the casing and narrowly recessed or "routed" on one side so it laps over the casing a little. Usually it is not moulded, merely has its edges rounded. In setting this, it will be mitered at the upper corners and in that way the unsightly end grain of the head casing is hidden. It will stop squarely on the window sill or, if it is a door casing, on the floor.

There are other ways to enrich trim. A simple one is to substitute a *moulded* casing, mitered at the top corners, for the old plain trim. This adds surprisingly to the general effect of the room. It might even throw the scheme off balance if the mantel in that room happened to be a very plain one. On the contrary, if there is a handsome mantel in a room that has plain door and window trim, merely adding a backband may not be sufficient enrichment; new, moulded, casings might be better. In the old days all mouldings were laboriously made by hand, using special planes which had cutters shaped to the desired curves. This was expensive, even in those days, so that sort of work was limited to rooms of special distinction, like the ballroom of Rich Tavern (Fig. 73). Today the local mill can supply well designed moulded casings at little cost.

Towards the end of the 1820's another casing fashion was developed which persisted for many years. Side casings of windows or doors, instead of being mitered with the head casing, were cut off on a line with its bottom, and the head casings were cut off on a line with the inside of the side casings. This left a square space in which a "corner block" was set. Usually this was a little thicker than the casing, so no neat fitting was needed. The block was set with the end grain on top, visible only to a fly on the ceiling whose feelings may be disregarded. A careful study of Figure 74 will suggest that these blocks were capable of a wide variety of ornamentation—they were never left plain. Late Victorian ones bore, as a rule, some pattern of concentric circles, far from admirable. As shown in the cut, the side casings often were treated like pilasters and provided with simple bases, usually better designed than those in the illustration.

Large, ornate houses with high ceilings need some sort of entablature above the door casing to give the desirable height to the composition without increasing that of the door itself (Fig. 75). The illustration shows the way in which the architect composed the interior design of this handsome room, using details that were in complete harmony with one another. The door casing is broken out around its top; above it is a plain frieze, then a fine cornice, its peculiar dentils deriving from the similar ones of another mantel in this house.

The room has a main cornice, of wood, with a plain frieze that is ornamented with triglyphs of a sort, flutes cut into its surface in groups of *four*—contradicting the Greek! The low wainscot adds the finishing touch to a room that is surprisingly stately for a Vermont farmhouse.

One of the amazing things about this house is its construction in a little over a year by three "ordinary" carpenters from the neighborhood, aided by the owner. And, as this was before the days of labor-saving machinery, all the fine work was done *by hand!* Equally amazing to us in these days when the struggle for status and its symbols may be distressing, is the true democracy of the men who built these mansions. A penniless orphan, the town apprenticed

73: RICH TAVERN, EAST MONTPELIER
Moulded door trim, wainscot

74: LEARNED HOUSE, TINMOUTH
Door trim with corner blocks

Joshua Munro to a shoemaker. Later he became a farmer with an unusual ability to make money. He amassed a fortune, raising, buying, and selling wheat at the time of the Napoleonic Wars, and built this handsome farm home. To the day of his death he not only worked in his fields, but made all the shoes needed by his family. He stayed a plain man.

The room shown in Figure 75 has three doors. One is the entrance from the

75: MUNRO-HAWKINS HOUSE, SHAFTSBURY
Ornate door-head, cornice in parlor

76: GOVERNOR GALUSHA HOUSE,
SHAFTSBURY
Chair rail, painted wall

hall, the other two flank the fireplace and its mantel. The two remaining walls have two fine windows each, their trim similar to that of the doors. Obviously, if the window scheme ended at the sill, it required some sort of base. This was made by continuing the sills to form the top of a low wainscot, a part of which shows in the cut. It is, of course, a good protection to the plaster which might otherwise be damaged by furniture, and also makes a very desirable base to the architectural composition.

A simple chair rail may give almost as good protection if its top is on a line with the window sills. The space between it and the baseboard may be so decorated that the effect is almost as satisfactory as a low wainscot. The one in the best bedroom of Governor Galusha's house (Fig. 76) seems lower than desirable for protection to the plaster. It shows the clever way the wall-painting was planned; the lower portion, below the chair rail, having a strongly horizontal movement in the design, that above it, rightly, emphasizing the vertical.

In some very old buildings a practical but not very ornamental low wainscot

77: PERKINS-WHITE HOUSE, WEST SHAFTSBURY
Ceiled wall, beamed ceiling

78: JONATHAN HUNT MANSION, VERNON
Paneled wainscot

was made with wide boards set horizontally, capped by a continuation of the round-edged window sill. In the Knight Tavern in Dummerston this not only runs around the halls of both first and second floor, but is carried up the stairs (Fig. 57) giving protection to the plaster of the wall if Boots was careless in carrying the guests' baggage. Oddly enough, in the handsome and sophisticated hallway of the Bradley House (Fig. 67) instead of carrying the wide-paneled low wainscot up the stairs, a substitute was made of rectangular pieces of the same panel boards in a curious stepped pattern, not very admirable for copying.

Most wainscot is paneled, a term that is frequently misused. A door, for example, consists of vertical stiles and horizontal rails. The rectangular spaces between them are the panels. In the oldest houses vertical planks were used for partitions, as already explained. Later on, similar construction was set on

79: HENRY HOUSE, BENNINGTON
Four paneled door, china cabinet

studding. These make a "ceiled" or "boarded" wall. Such a wall is not "paneled," nor is it wainscot. A "ceiled" wall, shown in Figure 77, had been hidden for many years under layers of wallpaper. After this was removed, it was neither difficult nor expensive to restore the wide, clear, pine boards to their

80: BURTON-CHASE HOUSE, THETFORD
Five paneled door, wainscot

original beauty. It is remarkable what results may be had by even unskilled hands using sandpaper, putty, and the right wood finish!

Paneled wainscot is very effective but expensive unless done by a home craftsman, who has no labor cost. The kind of panels used varies. Much old work was made with raised panels (Fig. 78) which avoids the use of mouldings. That sort has all four edges of the panels cut or tapered to a thinness that will fit into grooves that have been made in the edges of the stiles and rails. As far as effect goes, this takes the place of a moulding. Of course paneled wainscot, set against a wall, is seen on one side only. However, the doors of the same pattern that are in a paneled wall, are visible on both sides. Usually the back of the door has a flat panel, with or without a moulding according to the fancy of the maker. Raised panels must be made from solid wood. As the raised surface is about flush with that of the stiles and rails, the panel, if set in a 1/4-inch groove in the middle of a framework approximately an inch thick, will be of 1/2-inch stock. Few home craftsmen have the machine tools to make raised panels and must depend on some nearby mill, which will add to the cost of the work.

Paneled doors may be bought in a variety of designs from most lumber yards. Those with only four panels (Fig. 79) are not as pleasing as the six-panel pattern. There are two varieties of these. One has the small panels in the middle of the door's height (Fig. 80), which does not compose as well in most rooms as the so-called "Christian" doors with the small panels at the top (Fig. 75), which is, fortunately, the usual stock design. They may be bought with either raised or flat panels, the former costing a little more. There are two sorts of flat panel treatments. The better one to select has the edges of the styles and rails moulded (Fig. 72) rather than square (Fig. 76). A door without any panels at all is to be had, but its utter plainness is apt to destroy the scale of the doorway. Only the attractive but costly paneled wainscot has to be "made to order."

Flat paneled wainscot looks cheaper to the discerning eye, and it is. Its decorative effect may be increased with mouldings set in the angles between the framework and the panels, their corners neatly mitered. These mouldings must be bradded to the framework, not to the panel, in order to give the panels the needed opportunity to shrink and swell, moving with the humidity between winter and summer conditions. If the brads happen to pierce the panel, when the inevitable shrinkage occurs something has to give and usually the panel cracks. To obviate this, plywood may be used for flat panels. This comes in many thicknesses and is composed of from three to five layers of thin wood glued together under great pressure, their grains crossing. These layers are usually made of western fir, rotary cut, which means peeled off the log by tremendous razor-sharp knives. The unpleasantly coarse appearance of fir grain is offensive to many persons, and precludes using this material with a stained or varnished finish. Other woods are used also for plywood: pine, birch, mahogany, and the like. The rotary grain in some of these is less obtrusive, but still it is different from the flat grain of the framework wood.

Painted finish, then, is the solution of the problem, if plywood has to be used because the cost of solid wood is too great, or the panels too wide to be obtained in a solid material. This requires special treatment by the painter, but if properly sanded and coated with the right priming paint, the finished job cannot be told from one done with solid wood.

Flat panels are not as decorative as the raised variety. If the parts of the framework have square edges and there are no mouldings (Fig. 76) the appearance is rather dreary. If these edges are beveled, and the panel set farther in (Fig. 38) the improvement is marked. As already stated, it is still better if these edges are moulded (Fig. 72). If the framework edges are left square, the panel sunk still deeper and a good moulding placed around it, the appearance is almost as good as with raised panels, but it is a lot of work to cut, fit, and set all those mitered mouldings.

Generally speaking, wall-high paneled wainscot was confined to interior partitions, especially if a fireplace formed part of the composition. Examples of rooms with full-height paneled wainscot on all four sides are very rare in Early American houses. Usually a harmonizing low wainscot was used on the other three sides of the room. If a door was in part of the high wainscot, its panels were usually so arranged that its rails ranged with those of the wainscot (Fig. 78) as far as possible. In the cases where the housewright was careless in making his measurements, the failure to do this is distressing (Fig. 80). This picture also shows a wooden cornice moulding that softens the junction of the exposed timbers with the wall and ceiling but also a puzzling mantel design which arouses curiosity. It may have been a replacement of a former mantel, made at a later date by someone who was not sensitive to harmony.

Possibly it is not necessary to give a word of warning, that no wainscotting should be added to a room before new electric cables, other wiring, and heating or plumbing pipes have been considered and set in place. Of course they can be added out in plain view, but it is better to avoid this by a little foresight. Our forefathers did not have to consider those difficulties, but they did have a regard for using otherwise waste space for cupboards behind wainscot or in the similar paneling around chimneys. These will be noted in the preceding figures, and others may be seen in the illustrations of the chapter which deals with mantels. As far as known, these were always obvious. The secret panel or drawer, if any, is found only in furniture.

81: JONATHAN HUNT MANSION, VERNON
China cabinet, beamed ceiling

Decorative cabinets for the display of pewter and fine china were rare in Vermont's oldest houses. Some have been salvaged during the demolition of a half-ruined building and built in to another home, during alterations. Figure 79 is an example of such a fortunate preservation of a very simple but attractive specimen. The old curved shelves with their piecrust edges had to be set against the flat wall of the recess too shallow for the usual curved-back niche. It is in perfect keeping with the woodwork of the room, a former kitchen with its cavernous fireplace.

Another one was hidden behind a partition for many years before the lucky new owner discovered it while making repairs to falling plaster (Fig. 81). It is on the east wall of the room shown in Figure 78 and probably was originally set in similar wainscot. Some later owner apparently removed the wainscotting from this wall and cut a pass-pantry opening between this room and the adjoining kitchen, which accounts for the crude doors shown. The present owners made many discoveries and removed the boarded ceiling that had replaced the original plaster. Fortunately, the old pine had not been painted but had aged to a rich warm brown while hidden from view. The semicircular niche and half-dome set off the shelving and the front trim. Comparison of the two pictures also shows the improvement made by exposing the beams and girders.

Beamed ceilings have a great fascination for us today. It is perhaps a revulsion against the too-perfect white plaster, so cold and characterless. The heavy, widely spaced, hand-hewn beams of the old houses give a sense of security and comfort. They harmonize with a simple room, although they are not always in keeping with formal ones. But beamed ceilings are not invariably pleasing, especially if removal of plaster shows thin, deep floor timbers that are rough with marks of the saw. Also, such beams may be too close together for the scale of the room. They lack the character of "the real thing," hand-hewn and generous.

The effect may be bettered by placing a false ceiling of plaster below the newly exposed floor boards, hiding them. This will cover part of the beams, usually too deep and closer together than is desirable. This concealing plaster may be put on any backing, which in turn is furred down from the boards to the carefully considered distance for best appearance (Fig. 77). The usual

82: ROBINSON HOUSE, SOUTH READING
Unhewn beamed ceiling

plasterer will want to make this just as smooth and lacking in character as the plaster ceiling that has been taken away, and as a matter of course will use a tool called a "float." Only the most vigorous protests will persuade him to use a trowel or a very short float. With that, it is almost impossible to get a smooth surface. It will wave a little, show a few toolmarks. He will be horrified, but that is what the effect should be! Then, instead of leaving it white, or painting it like the walls, prime it (after it is thoroughly dry) with a cheap varnish, thinned a little, and follow with a second coat. This should result in a fine old-ivory color that varies quite a little from one part to another of the long thin "panel" between the beams, yet is not mottled. If this is a truly old house, why not make the plaster between the beams look as if it had been done by the original owner, maybe a century and a half ago? It has been said that "dirt is matter out of place," but if it has come to be in the right places through the long years, we call it "patina" and admire it.

Many really old farmhouses had hand-hewn girders, but sometimes the floor beams were just round logs of the proper thickness and spacing, their tops smoothed off to receive the floor boards of the second story (Fig. 82). In an evidently very old house with utterly simple interior detail, the plaster ceiling may be removed and the old beams of this sort exposed with a happy result. Here is where a little imagination should be used before any drastic ceiling demolition is begun. "All things are right, but not all things are expedient." In other words, better a plaster ceiling than one with beams that may be right from the engineering standpoint but wrong from that of the decorator.

Suppose the plaster ceiling has been removed, exposing to view really good hand-hewn beams. Probably they, and the under sides of the flooring they carry, will be dirty and need some sort of treatment. Frequently brushing will be enough, even if a wire brush has to be used. If the project includes removal of plaster from an old plank partition, its surface may call for smoothing down a bit to remove some of the saw marks. This may be done with a small power sander, held in the hand, which will leave the wood lighter than the other parts. If there is a boarded wall, some new boards may be required, and these will have to be toned or "equalized," as finishers say, to match the others. The same is true of the floor boards which replace old ones.

In one such case the owner found that the excellent hewn beams were of red oak, and the planks of white pine. The colors clashed, even if modified by age, but by following a method known to those who restore antiques, a perfectly satisfactory result was attained. The method depends somewhat on what effect is wanted. If it is to make the wood look like the *unfinished* old work, experiment with kerosene as a vehicle, coloring it with "color-in-oil" of various sorts. These come in tubes to be had at any paint store, and as very small amounts are needed the small size will suffice. A mixture may be made (by trial and error) of yellow ochre, burnt siena, and lampblack, blended with a putty knife, and small amounts added at a time to the kerosene. Sop it on to a sample piece with a brush, let it dry about ten or fifteen minutes, then rub off with a rough cloth (an old Turkish towel is good). Making several samples, each with an identifying number that agrees with the little containers', let it dry overnight. It may be found considerably lighter next morning. Generous applications of this to the work, keeping it lighter than wanted so a second or even third coat will give the desired result on the lightest part of the work, will bring success. The smell of kerosene will soon disappear, but the wood will have the characteristics of any *unfinished* wood and cannot be scrubbed if real dirt, not "patina," makes unsightly spots.

If the owner's desire is for a finish that can be really cleaned with soap and water, one that is similar to a "natural" floor finish is required. The most satisfactory is one of the new "penetrating oil finish" type referred to under the discussion of floors later in this chapter. This needs a little more experience, but by following the same sequence, a first coat containing stain but quite light, followed if needed by a second coat of corrective color or intensity and a final coat of the clear material, a permanent result is attained. The kerosene-based stain will darken with age and sunlight very considerably, while the "oil finish," being a sort of varnish, will not change much. The success of this latter finish depends on following the directions on the can—the only catch being to learn by experience *when* the proper amount of penetration or drying has occurred and the amount of the material to be wiped off. Even professional painters are apt to err, as few have had experience with this good but somewhat tricky material. When done right, the result is much more pleasing than the normal stain-and-varnish treatment used by professional painters whose admiration for the slick and perfect is out of keeping with the old work. It is hard for them to understand why some persons prefer the individuality and variety of handwork to the even perfection of the machine.

Floors may worry the restorer. Chapter II has a good deal about those used in old times, and the attic, or in some cases even the barn, may furnish suitable material. Modern floors are made of narrow tongued and grooved wood and of various materials. Spruce is usually confined to attics. White pine is seldom used except in very special wide widths that are costly. Oregon fir, unless edge grain is specified, is apt to splinter, and beech is hard to get. Maple is so very hard and dense that it does not absorb stain or hold paint well, besides being expensive. Oak is more "thankful" to the finisher and comes in a wide price range depending on whether it is red or white oak, flat grain or quartered. It is also sold in "ready-finished" packaged flooring.

In finishing a floor it is always debatable whether to keep it as light as possible or to stain it. Many feel that a floor, as the base or foundation of a decorative scheme, should be dark, an excellent background for whatever furniture or rugs may be used. The purpose of the room usually clarifies the situation. The Victorian fashion for covering an entire floor, wall to wall, with a carpet of some sort, has its adherents. This may be laid on a cheap spruce floor. Its disadvantages hardly need to be mentioned and it certainly is undesirable for bedrooms and halls, and quite ridiculous for a kitchen, in which linoleum has practical advantages that are obvious.

If a floor is to be finished "natural," one of the newer penetrating oil finishes previously mentioned is very satisfactory. It is almost the only thing to use on an old floor that has worn to a rather wavy surface from the friction of many feet through the years. It is especially good for a modern oak floor, as it will sink into the pores better than any other material and has the very great advantage of being a finish that can be patched when wear has caused light spots. A varnished floor cannot be patched. It has to be sanded and scraped down to the original bare wood, restained, primed, and then varnished. Many of the modern varnishes may be had in a flat or egg-shell gloss, preferable to the shiny sort if a trifle less durable. If varnish is used, a preliminary priming coat of shellac is frequently used. This is not as good as the primer of the varnish intended for the finished coats that has been diluted with turpentine or some other thinner as directed on the can. This will assure a similarity of "coefficient of expansion" during changes of temperature and will wear better. Floor varnishes are made from different materials than those intended for furniture or standing trim, which are not suitable for the heavy wear-and-tear of traffic, nor so resistant to spotting from water.

In old days all standing trim was painted, unless, as in a few examples, left without any finish coat whatever. Floors were very seldom of hardwood, and when it was used, as in ballrooms, it was waxed. Softwood floors, as in some of the old taverns, were left without any finish and were scrubbed and in some cases sprinkled with sand—a great convenience to tobacco chewers! The early homemade paints would not stand up under traffic, and when oil paint was developed that would serve for floors it must have been a welcome aid to housewives. These specially compounded floor paints have been steadily improved

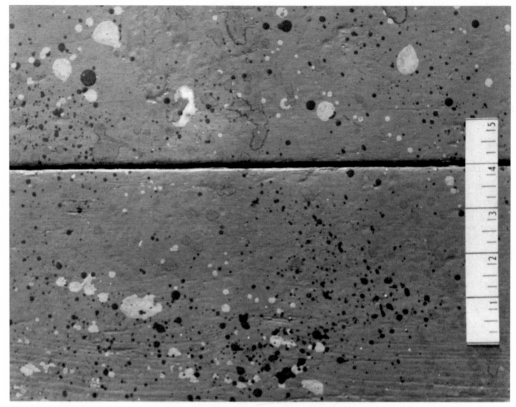

83: RED COTTAGE, WEST ARLINGTON
Spatter-dash floor painting

and are now durable, easy to apply, and cheaper than any other finish. Because of the great increase in the cost of hardwood flooring, cheaper woods, like Oregon fir, are popular and are usually painted. Of course, for old houses, wide boards look better than the narrow strips of modern flooring—if they can be had.

During the nineteenth century ingenious housewives invented "spatter-dash" floor painting and it was widely used, especially for informal sitting rooms and bedrooms. When it is well done a floor of this sort has a great deal of character and can change a room from dullness to comeliness. As its name suggests, it is a purposeful spattering with paint of a contrasting color on the ground color of the floor (Fig. 83). Perhaps it originated from a careless person

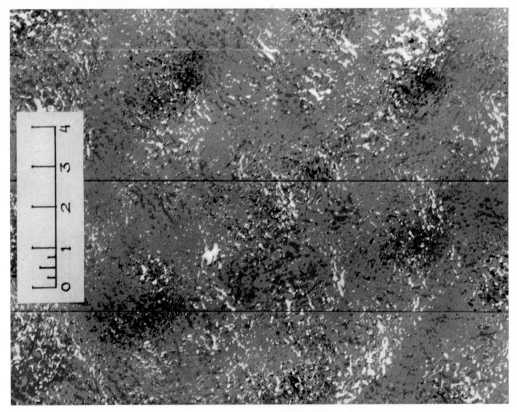

84: H. W. CONGDON HOUSE, ARLINGTON
Textured floor painting

dripping spots of paint from an overcharged brush, but with practise it became an art for the skilful, something that could be done by a woman of imagination, glad to help her busy farmer-husband. The early examples all show black or very dark spots on a ground of gray that varies from light to a dull bluish-lead color. Later, the contrast was reversed, with a dark floor spattered in two or more light colors, adding gaiety to the effect. It was just difficult enough to do well that with changing fashions it became almost a lost art. Like some other old skills, it is now coming back again.

A minor art, it can be learned by doing; the book merely gives suggestions. The first of these is to use only a good floor paint. Enamels do not work as well, they are more expensive, do not wear any better, and are, to many tastes, too shiny. The second is to be sure the ground color is thoroughly dry and hard before beginning the work. This should have been applied, following the directions on the can, with a good bristle brush in the usual manner. For the finishing "spots" do not use a bristle brush but an ordinary whisk broom, the old-fashioned kind made of broomcorn. This will hold paint better and drop spots and splatters of more uniform size and altogether be easier to control. Pour some of the spotting paint in a pan, dip the tip of the whisk broom in it, and experiment, preferably on some spread out newspapers, for the first trials are apt to be unsuccessful. The broom should not be overcharged but of course must be sufficiently filled so that drops will fall readily, although judicious shaking will vary their size and number. The paint must be thoroughly stirred, but only trial will determine whether or not it should be diluted. If this is necessary, use turpentine or mineral spirits as directed on the can.

If more than one color is to be used for the spots, the first set must be given time to become dry and hard. An especially wet spot may not dry overnight and, if pasty, would smear when stepped on. If two colors are used for spots, only experiment will tell which forms the first set. On a rich brown ground the spots might be of bright yellow and blue, or red, or all three. Some protection will be needed for baseboards, as the spattering must be done close to the edge of the floor for good effect. Floor decoration of this sort is a job for the "do-it-yourself" person because of labor cost. It is well worth the effort and would complete a restoration rewardingly.

An easier but not quicker method has been developed which gives a somewhat similar textured effect but requires very little skill—only time, like the old authentic one. It, also, starts with a suitable foundation color applied in the usual manner and given time to become thoroughly dry. Where the old way uses two or three sets of spots dripped from a whisk broom, this easier method applies the dabs of color with pads of steel wool. The paint is not in a deep pan, but a wet coat is applied to a sort of palette like a square of tin, the pad wetted on it and applied like a rubber stamp. The first color should be dabbed in an open pattern, leaving room for the second set and the third can partly cover these as well as the ground color between the previous spots (Fig. 84). These spots will dry hard faster than the dripped ones. Usually they will be ready after an overnight drying, so the work may be completed sooner than with the

85: ROBINSON HOUSE, SOUTH READING
Stencilled wall painting

old method. The effect is softer when done the new way—preference is a matter of taste. Rubber gloves should be worn to protect the hands. Regardless of which method is used, after the floor is dry and hard it is wise to apply a coat of a light-colored floor varnish for protection.

These decorated floors are not very common. The majority of rooms were done with solid color and make an excellent background for old-fashioned rag or hooked rugs. Surprisingly, they seem to be as satisfactory for Oriental or Navajo ones!

Wall treatments fall in three classes. Wainscotting has been discussed, wallpaper is not in the province of this book, but the third, painting, is the traditional method for our old houses. Bare plaster soon gets dirty and is so utterly neutral at best that it is only natural that some decoration is desirable. In very early farmhouses homemade paint was applied, the commonest being lime whitewash. Long ago this was found to be more permanent if milk was added to it— the first use of what is now a casein paint. Some farms had "paint" deposits, small patches of colored clays that the Indians had used, called red or yellow ochre. These could be used as tinting colors in whitewash. With the later availability of oil paints a greater variety of interior decoration was made possible to those whose prosperity and taste desired it. Door and window casings might be painted with white lead, walls with the old tinted lime wash, or the color contrast reversed. Those who have visited the Early American rooms in city museums or our excellent Shelburne Musem in Vermont are familiar with another, more serene treatment, with walls and wood trim all of the same delicate color, often a pale gray-blue. Modern rubber-base paints come in a wide variety of suitable colors and are easy to apply with brush or roller without the expense of a professional painter and they have the great advantage of being washable.

Here varying tastes come into conflict, the modern with the traditional. Discussion of taste is fruitless, as the old Latin adage reminds us. If the traditional is to win, it must be on the score of conservatism, of the love of things as they have always been. The architecture of Early American houses does not take kindly to the frenetic brilliance of much of the ultra-modern coloring which is illustrated in the "home decoration" magazines. Whether the new owner has bought a dwelling for year-round occupancy or as a summer home, it is often as a refuge from the breathlessness of suburban or city life. The serenity of an old house should be retained, perhaps, and "exciting new ideas" kept for other architectural styles.

Before wallpaper was available, our forebears enriched plastered walls with stencilled ornamentation, usually in quiet colorings (Fig. 85), done by traveling specialists in this sort of work. They came equipped with a wide variety of patterns capable of combination in a number of ways, so no two rooms looked alike even if the stencil elements might identify the worker. This sort of wall decoration is certainly appropriate today for ornamentation of hallways and even whole rooms. It is possible for an enthusiast to produce excellent results on a "do-it-yourself" basis if a little research is done. One of the modern books, Janet Waring's *Early American Wall Stencils,* would be a fine source of ideas for designs and colors. The color plates in that and other similar books cover this fascinating field admirably. It is not difficult to make stencils, and their careful use would permit several colors to be applied in one operation. Figures 58 and 61 show a larger expanse of stencil work, but a pleasing effect may be had by limiting the stencilling to a strip at the top of the wall, softening the harsh break between it and the ceiling. Wall treatment of this sort may be liked by some as a permanency, while others would condemn it for the same reason.

Wallpaper came into common use during the reign of Queen Victoria and, as methods of its manufacture were improved and its cost lowered, superseded other forms of wall treatment. The early and very expensive landscape paper, found only in the homes of the wealthy, is not within the scope of this book. Perhaps the entire subject of wallpaper should be omitted, except for the fact that successive layers of paper, mostly undesirable, served to cover and preserve treatments now considered valuable. Today, everyone realizes that new paper should not be pasted on old, and while removing even a single layer is a messy job, it is done gladly when the old paper is ugly or in bad condition. There is enough unworthy wallpaper shown in the illustrations of excellent interior trim and mantels in this book to make it plain that commendation of the wallpaper is not included in that of the woodwork! The illustrations should be looked at selectively. Aristophanes was quite right when he said "Happy is the man possessed of a taste accurate, refined, and chaste."

86: MUNRO-HAWKINS HOUSE, SHAFTSBURY
"Chimneys 'gainst the sky"

[VII]

CHIMNEYS

————◆·◉·◆————

FEW REALIZE the importance of chimneys as decorative elements of house design. If suitably designed in mass, proportion, and location they are valuable accents against the skyline, relieving the monotony of the horizontal lines of eaves and ridge. Moreover, they identify the building as a home. Consider Joshua Munro's mansion (Fig. 86) and imagine what it would look like if there were no visible chimneys. It is a stately building, but without them might be taken for the administration building of some centrally heated institution instead of a dwelling. With them, it is obviously a home. This decorative quality is combined with the functional. A chimney must serve the practical necessity of carrying away smoke and gaseous products of combustion. It must do this work efficiently and safely, for the comfort and even the lives of the occupants of the dwelling depend on this practical need. Too many old houses have been destroyed by fires due to defective flues, for our forefathers did not always use precautions in construction that we know now are essential to safety. This chapter deals with restoration and repair after the very necessary inspection that is also described. Suggestions are also made for complete rebuilding in those cases where former chimneys have been demolished. The next chapter describes suitable fireplace construction.

Most of our oldest houses were built with a single massive central chimney around which its rooms clustered (Figs. 1, 18). This was at first what might be called a "Santa Claus" type, with one huge shaft or flue into which smaller ones opened, originating in the various fireplaces of the first floor and, sometimes, the cellar. Some of these dwellings were of the story-and-a-half sort, and the bedrooms in the upper portion (if any) were unheated. If it was a storage attic, there might be an opening into the chimney (closed by a thick plank door) to permit meats to be smoked there, hung on iron hooks set in the flue wall. This big chimney, its bulky mass rising well above the roof, was seldom without its hospitable wisp of smoke, the "hearthfire smoke against the sky" beloved of the poets. Later chimneys, especially those that have been rebuilt, have separate fireplace flues within them which prevent the down drafts that were inevitable with the big shafts. These also strengthen the masonry and lessen the erosion of the brickwork.

An inevitable inconvenience of the house plan with rooms clustered about a central chimney was the cramped entrance hall and resulting uncomfortable staircase (Figs. 65, 66). Efforts towards overcoming these defects were largely responsible for the development of the plan with central hall between pairs of rooms which, consequently, had at least two chimneys. Smaller houses with the entrance at the *end* of the house had the hall at one side and, therefore, could get along with only one chimney and still have a comfortable stairway and entrance hall.

The larger houses, those with a central hall flanked by pairs of rooms, had two or four chimneys, depending on the location of their fireplaces. These might be set against the longitudinal partitions separating the front from the back rooms, which meant two chimneys which would pierce the roof in the neighborhood of, or at, the ridge, as in Figure 86. They could also be set against the end walls of the rooms. In this case, if the house were large and its front and back rooms big enough to require a fireplace in each room, there would be four chimneys, two at each end, as in Figure 16. In smaller dwellings of this type the rooms behind the front ones were apt to be smaller and unheated. This permitted one chimney at each end of the house, its fireplace set off center on the end wall of the room (Fig. 87). This resulted in an unsymmetrical composition of the end of the house, although its front remained formal and symmetrical, an arrangement also seen in the Ebenezer Robinson addition (Fig. 8). In the case of a small house set with its main entrance on the long side, but one end facing the street and therefore considered the "front," two chimneys might be set at that end, in a symmetrical grouping, the true front, with its entrance, being unsymmetrical (Fig. 88). This may seem beside the point to

87: ALGER HOUSE, GRAFTON
End chimneys, off center

those seeking help in making a restoration of an old house, but is of value in showing the different ways in which the old master builders solved their problems.

The condition and construction of the chimneys of an old house should be matters of serious concern to the family dwelling there and of first importance to a purchaser. Fire is a terrible master as well as a necessary and sometimes treacherous servant. Insurance statistics show many household tragedies due to what is casually described as "a defective flue." Because the chimney stack is

88: BATSTONE HOUSE, SOUTH LONDONDERRY
Twin chimneys at one end only

almost completely hidden, its safety is taken for granted both by householders and those looking for a desirable purchase. Leaky roofs are easily repaired, rotted sills may be replaced without great expense, but few persons, whether residents or buyers, think of chimneys as the greatest hazard to life in what seems otherwise a very desirable home. Anyone driving along country highways or byways with an eye out for old houses may see, if he looks, many a chimney with a ragged top from which bricks have vanished, plainly indicating that the flue walls are dangerously thin and its mortar joints weakened. To be sure, sometimes these are new "tops" built cheaply, and the parts of the chimney below the roof may be more safely constructed. A safe chimney is more important than a tight roof or a solid frame. Durability in its exposed part and a proper height, in scale with the house, are next in importance.

Thorough inspection of chimneys should begin at the fireplaces. Poor draft, evidenced by smoke stains on a mantel, may be due to an ill-laid fire or a dirty chimney, temporary conditions. It is wise to look up the chimney from a fireplace, and "they do it with mirrors" is a hint, not a joke. Thickness of flue walls may be measured at a stovepipe hole, if any, and there, too, a mirror may show the condition of the flue above. At that vantage point one may check for the desirable terra-cotta flue linings, which make even a four-inch-thick flue wall reasonably safe. If the flue has been lined merely with a thin plastering of mortar on the interior surface, there is a strong probability that this will crack, sheet off, and reduce the flue area, making proper cleaning difficult. The mirror may show chimney-swift nests glued to the side of the flue, as well as incrustations of that black and sticky substance called creosote, which under certain conditions is highly inflammable.

The next step in inspection is to view the chimney above the ceiling of the top floor and under the slope of the roof. In houses with very flat pitched roofs this may mean crawling over ceiling beams. Boards laid across the beams will make it easier and prevent sticking a toe through the ceiling below! If one knows the number and sizes of flues it is easy to calculate the thickness of the chimney walls, remembering that the "withes" or partitions between flues are normally only four inches thick.

Finally, look at the chimney top. In good construction this should be either a solid slab of stone pierced for the flues or a cast cement one. Often, that part has grown insecure and has been replaced, too often with some plain or fancy *brick* topping. It is important that the cap be waterproof, either of stone or cast-in-place cement with waterproofing in the mix.

Bricks, even the hard-burned ones, absorb an amazing quantity of water. A prolonged rain will soak them, and the moisture will settle down by gravity, until second-floor rooms where the chimneys have plastered surfaces may show stains on the wall paper. This is not a roof leak that can be checked by proper metal "flashing" or repointing mortar in the chimney above the roof. The only sure way to stop this trouble is to give that part of the brickwork a couple of coats of one of the transparent waterproofing solutions, available at building-material stores. Despite the effects of weather, this will protect it for many years. But do not *paint* a handsome piece of brick masonry. Choose a good hard-burned common brick of excellent color, lay the bricks in cement mortar that includes waterproofing material in its mix, and let the mason use good full joints pointed flush with the brick.

All of that attention to chimneys is vitally important to the family that has lived in the old house for several generations and hopes their children and grandchildren will continue there. It also applies to the new owner.

If the inspection shows unlined flues (lacking flue linings) the chimney is as dangerous as a rattlesnake and will give no warning, as that reptile does, before disaster strikes. Oh yes, there might be a smell of smoke, but that might come from other, natural, causes. If the lower part of the chimney has eight inches of brick around the flues, but only four inches above the roof, take the chimney down to where it meets the eight-inch walls and rebuild it with eight-inch walls *and* flue linings, from below roof to top. It will look better and need less upkeep. Compare Figure 49 with Figure 16.

If it is found that only four inches of brickwork surrounds old unlined flues, the whole chimney must be torn down as far as the fireplace throats of the ground floor. And if there is a cellar fireplace, such as are found in some old houses, where soap was made, that could be bricked up. Rebuilding properly will cost money, but so do funerals, and they cost more than mere money. Better be safe than be sorry.

Some chimneys may hide fire-danger spots that cannot be found by any reasonable inspection. One owner, who wanted to replace a Victorian marble mantel with something in keeping with his house, had an architect inspect the chimney, built in 1830 and, as far as could be seen, in perfect condition. Much against his will, the owner accepted the advice of his suspicious architect and went to a considerable expense, tearing the chimney down from its top to the smoke chamber of the ground-floor fireplace. The four-inch flue walls seemed in fairly good condition, and the owner was a bit resentful until the demolition reached the second floor. There, it was found that the unlined flue walls, close to the fireplace, were full of leaks. Still worse, the main girder that supported the second-floor beams was built *into* the chimney and carried by the four inches of brickwork that had lost most of its mortar. The end of the timber was exposed to the great heat of the oil-burner draft and was charred for several feet between the floor and parlor ceiling, completely out of sight but directly under the twin beds used by his children. Only good luck had saved them from fiery deaths. The chimney was rebuilt from the ground-floor fireplace up, using flue linings *and* eight inches of brick around them all the way to the top. The matter of expense was not mentioned again.

The operation was a comparatively simple one. The chimney was at the end of the house and built entirely inside the frame according to the excellent old custom, so no part of the exterior was affected, only a bit of plastering. If the chimney is a central one with rooms and their fireplaces clustered around it, a rebuilding is more disturbing as well as costly. Figures 7 and 82 show the difficulties met in rebuilding the chimney in the Robinson house, in which one room had wall-high boarding and all three fireplaces had to be retained in their original condition. It needed ingenuity and collaboration between the owner and his almost heroic mason. The owner described the proceedings in *Vermont Life* (Vol. II, No. 3) from which the following is quoted:

"Down came the chimney to its junction with the three fireplace openings, without disturbing a single plank of the wide pine panelling (*sic*). The chimney was rebuilt with flue linings, and the old hand-made bricks of lovely color and texture. The mason did all his work standing *inside* the big chimney." It is to be hoped that he was slender as well as agile!

It is a much simpler operation to rebuild a chimney from the attic floor to its top when the shaft is straight. If a bend is necessary, the new work should make the slope as long and gentle as possible under the existing conditions. Flue linings should be used of course. If the chimney has only four-inch walls where it comes through the attic floor, they should be increased to eight inches thick before passing through the roof. As previously stated, rain-soaked bricks may spall if they freeze during the night, and the natural erosion of even the best mortar makes the thicker walls desirable, so the bricks may be "bonded" and not depend solely on the adhesion of the mortar. "Bonding" means that even if most of them are laid lengthways of the wall, every so often a brick is laid as a "header," with its length at right angles to the others, thus tying the two four-inch layers of brick together. The top or cap of the chimney should be, as stated earlier, either a single stone slab pierced for the flues or of cast-in-place cement of a waterproof mix, which may be gently tapered from its bed to its top surface. Some brickmasons like to top out with a row of bricks set on end. This is extremely good looking, but in a few years frost and weather erosion of the mortar may work them loose. Their fall may damage the roof. Such a topping may be attractive to look at, but it does not waterproof the brickwork beneath it, another reason that it is undesirable.

Even casual inspection may show that a chimney needs cleaning. Like many other maintenance jobs, this will be of little interest to a prospective buyer, but once the house is bought it should be a routine procedure, all the more necessary if the dwelling is not a new one but a longtime home. Chimney fires occur only in *dirty* chimneys, and there is no especial rule for the frequency of this unpleasant task. Like the small boy who sees no use in washing his hands before supper because he had an all-over scrub when he got up that morning, the average householder lets a disagreeable job wait.

Some day a bigger fire than usual may have been kindled in the most frequently used fireplace. Perhaps the faded Christmas greens are being burned, or the children, fascinated by the glowing sparks on the encrusted fireback ("people going to church"), may throw some birchbark or paper on the burning logs. Bigger flames roar up the chimney. Suddenly the inflammable creosote crust in the chimney throat (the lower part of the flue) is ignited and you have a chimney fire. You may want the fire department—if there is one. The noise is terrifying. The chimney belches a huge column of smoke and flame from its top. Burning pieces of crust fall into the fireplace. Smoke may fill the room. Open a window to increase the draft in order to keep the smoke out of the room, if possible. Throw on handfuls of ordinary table salt to reduce the flames. If you are brave enough, let it burn, and you will have a thoroughly cleaned chimney! But first make a trip to the attic and feel the exposed brickwork. If it is too hot to touch, or if your chimney lacks flue linings, and especially if the floating, flaming crusts fall outdoors on dry grass and start fires, use the telephone *fast*. With *eight* inches of brick around the flues that adjoin stud partitions, even without flue linings, and with roofs covered by slate instead of a flammable material, there is not much chance of disaster to the house. The danger, then, is from the flaming pieces outdoors, settling on wooden roofs of outbuildings, in dead leaves, in dry grass. A winter or rainy-day chimney fire is the least dangerous, and the greatest harm will come from loss of reputation, for good housekeepers do not have such fires.

Cleaning a chimney is still a trade. Even the flue that serves an oil burner is safer if regularly cleaned. Bituminous coal, also, differing from anthracite, leaves inflammable soot in the chimney and so does softwood. Lacking a professional chimney sweep, it is not really a difficult job, but a very dirty one. An adventurous and sure-footed twelve-year-old boy has done it. He got out of a dormer window and crawled up the roof, wearing rubber-soled sneakers. Playing Santa Claus seemed rather good fun but instead of wearing a pack he had a length of clothes line leading back to the dormer. Astride of the chimney top he hauled up the rope. On the end of it was an old burlap bag packed with hay in which were a lot of stones, rather a loose fit for the flue. The bag was lowered down the chimney, a little way at a time, scrubbing it up and down, then lowering it farther and repeating the scrubbing. This was continued until the "scrubbing bag" reached the fireplace below, preceded by showers of soot, crusts, and chimney-swift nests. Much of this lodged on the wind-shelf, and the throat damper had to be removed to get it all out. There was plenty of dirt on the hearth for the master of the house to sweep up. Then on to the next flue! Considering the fragility of roofing slates it is really a job for a careful boy rather than his heavier parent. Perhaps it is not an ideal do-it-yourself job. The soot and other material that has been removed is an excellent dressing for the garden. It should not be wasted.

Brick laying, also, is not a do-it-yourself craft. While many of the old framed houses were built and even finished by farmer-craftsmen, the mason work seems to have been done by professionals even in those days. They were well-trained men who had passed through the stages of apprentice, journeyman, and master craftsman. One of their methods of construction, which has been mentioned before, was to leave at least an inch of air space between hewn timbers and chimney masonry. That precaution saved many old structures from destruction by fire, for, with all their good workmanship, they did take chances with the thickness of flue walls. Flue linings were unknown until comparatively recent times and there were no Building Codes. Today, improperly supervised workmen and uninformed owners build chimneys that would displease the old housewrights.

Too many worthy old houses have had *outside* chimneys added to the detriment of their design. In old Vermont houses, as elsewhere in New England, the chimneys were always built entirely *within* the frame. If they were on end walls, they were concealed until they appeared above the roof, where they were essential parts of the architectural composition. Building an *outside* chimney as a replacement for one that has been removed is a grave error. Not only does it damage the balance of a formal design, but it has the practical shortcoming of being completely exposed to the weather, which entails more upkeep expense, like repointing mortar joints. Also, the cold of winter chills the air in the flues. Cold air falls, so down drafts are stronger and chillier than in a chimney which has a large part of its masonry warmed by the interior temperature. It is more difficult to kindle a fire in the fireplace without having it smoke, for the same reason. Finally, despite its acceptance in the picturesque and dubiously Colonial cottages of Suburbia, it is out of place on an old house of formal design.

Replacing fireplaces and their chimneys that have been removed in the course of former "improvements" should be done only after a study of the framing of the ground floor as seen on the cellar ceiling or, if the building is one of the "never-was-it" class, after careful thought of the exterior appearance. Preceding pages should help in this. The next chapter deals with the proper sizes of flues in proportion to the fireplace openings in order to provide adequate draft, for a smoky fireplace is a nuisance. Equally important, however, is the height of the chimney. If located at the ridge, the cap should never be less than two feet above it—as illustrated in several of the pictures. If the chimney pierces the roof farther down the slope, the height above the ridge should be increased to avoid down drafts.

The restorer will find that attention to the three practical elements, chimney height, flue area, and fireplace opening, is vital to the attainment of the other three; beauty, comfort, and efficiency.

[VIII]

FIREPLACES

WHEN PRIMITIVE man tamed fire he made his first step towards civilization. He soon began to love it for its cheer quite as much as its warmth, and that strong liking stays with us. Perhaps it has been pushed down into a subconscious level as we have found more efficient ways of cooking our food and heating our homes, yet we have a fellow feeling for the unregenerate heathen who cried out, "Aha, I am warm, I have seen the fire!" Apartment-house dwellers may pound on cold steam pipes, but when the surly janitor raises the boiler pressure, who would exclaim joyfully, "I have seen the radiator"? No. We want to see the leaping flames, to "smell birch smoke at twilight," and the most important feature of that "little place in the country" is its fireplace.

The open fire is a beloved anachronism. At best it is a source of supplementary heat in winter even if the efficient but unromantic oil burner can keep every room in the house at a predetermined temperature. Nevertheless, it has its usefulness on chilly mornings, even in midsummer, when firing the central-heating system would overheat the rooms by noon. Its warmth is more than physical on a frosty autumn evening or when winter gales drive the snow against the window panes. To be sure, wood fuel is costly if it has to be bought, but if the place has a few weed trees or a very small wood lot where there is downwood that is better burned in the fireplace than on a bonfire, the fuel cost is trivial. It drops to zero if the householder believes the old Vermont adage that wood from your own wood lot heats you twice, once when you work it up, again when you burn it. Woods differ widely in their fitness for fireplace use. There seems to be a direct connection between their specific gravity and the B.T.U. content. In other words, a piece of dry wood that is very heavy will give more heat when burned than one of the same size that is very light. Some woods burn quietly, others are explosive and snap when burning, throwing out sparks that are a fire hazard unless held back by a fire screen. Woods as fuel will be discussed in Chapter X.

Fireplaces that are still in use in various parts of the world differ greatly in design. There are remote farmhouses in Iceland, for example, where the bee-hive-shaped kitchen, built of lava slabs, has a circular hearth raised a few inches from the stone floor. On this a peat fire smoulders, its acrid smoke rising to a circular opening in the top of the domed stone ceiling. In some of the old manor houses in England the log-fire on the hearth is backed by the stone walls of the hall and has a beautifully carved hood several feet above it, the smoke escaping through a huge flue sheltered by the hood. These archaic affairs need no further consideration. This book deals only with the typical Early American fireplaces as built from pre-Revolutionary times onward to their abandonment when stoves made them obsolete. The owner of one of these old houses may have to rebuild the chimney, but it would be foolish to change the old fireplace and its hearth if it is still in place. Sometimes it has been covered up, semi-permanently, and only needs to be brought to sight, and use, again.

In some cases the original kitchen fireplace was left when the others were removed, or modernized with inharmonious Victorian mantels. It may be identi-fied by the old-fashioned oven, generally built at one side of the very wide, high fireplace. Few would care to do serious cooking there, but if the oven is still flue-connected it will be found a treasure for baking beans or even bread and rolls. To bake in such an oven is truly an art, not an easily mastered science like the use of our modern ones with their thermostats and accurately controlled heat. A few adventurous housewives have experimented (Fig. 89), to the great pleasure of their families, by the simple expedient of testing the heat with a modern oven thermometer.

The method is simple enough, even if strange to us today. A small fire is built with dry wood in the middle of the oven floor, using little split sticks about a foot long. When it seems to be well kindled, the opening is closed with a plug (not shown in the cut) like a square cover, faced with metal on the inside, until the brickwork gets thoroughly heated up. That, of course, does have to be a

89: WOODWARD-GRAZIANO HOUSE,
CASTLETON
Using an old built-in oven

matter of guesswork at first. Then the glowing coals are raked down into the ashpit beneath, the temperature tested by oven thermometer, the food put in, and the plug re-inserted. The brickwork will hold its heat for an amazingly long time, with very little drop during the first hour or so. With baked beans the temperature drop is rather an advantage because long, slow baking improves them. Originally, most of these ovens and ashpits had plate-iron doors and latches, which were easier to use.

A good many of the old kitchen fireplaces that have come down to us almost unchanged exposed the greater part of the chimney breast, the mantel being an irreducible minimum of woodwork. The corners of the openings were of brick or stone but the hearth was almost always of brick (Fig. 90). The crane was long enough for several pots or kettles to be hung from it, their height above the fire regulating cooking from "full rolling boil" to "simmer" according to the number and length of the pothooks (shaped like long S's) by which they were suspended and their distance from the liveliest part of the fire. Contrary to usual belief, these big, high fireplaces did not use huge logs. The rather thin firewood

90: "THE MAPLES," CASTLETON
Former kitchen fireplace

was generally leaned, up-and-down, against a backlog that smoldered all day. Cooking was not dissimilar from the way woods-folk cook on a campfire, the length of the fire varying from a small spot to a long thin one according to need. Naturally the brick facing accumulated what we may politely call "patina," yet was kept decently clean. Given high-grade hard-burned bricks, sometimes burned from the farm clay pit, the color is very beautiful. To paint or plaster such treasures (Fig. 78) is a grievous error. In more ornate homes, the kitchen mantel was slightly elaborated and enriched by covering the oven openings with paneled doors (Fig. 91). Now many of these former kitchens have become dining rooms and are in keeping with the decor of a simple, informal family room, "a place for quiet mirth and storytelling."

Nothing has been mentioned so far about corner fireplaces. There are good

91: BEN HULETT HOUSE, SHAFTSBURY
Kitchen fireplace; door covers oven

reasons why this type is so rare in Vermont. It is less efficient as a heating apparatus and it is upsetting to the usual composition of a room in the Colonial style. In this, the accent, or focus of interest, belongs in the middle of a wall. A corner fireplace puts it on a diagonal of the rectangle, which is the normal floor plan. A good deal depends on the way the old-time master builder thought about locating his chimneys—whether their place in the exterior composition was more important than the situation of the fireplaces they served, or the other way around. If he wanted to have two ground-floor rooms at the end of the

92: WOODMAN HOUSE, WEST ARLINGTON
Corner fireplace in living room

plan and a single chimney about on the line of the longitudinal partition, corner fireplaces for these rooms was an obvious solution of his problem. Of course it would be impossible to have a formal, balanced composition for these rooms. Most of the real old-timers would not accept such a solution, but about 1840 a few did not feel that this was important.

One of the best corner fireplaces has a mantel treatment that makes its position in the room not only tolerable, but charming (Fig. 92). It seems, from the treatment above the mantel shelf, as if the smoke chamber and flue were centered with the fireplace opening and sloped back to the chimney, which is in its normal position. The lines of the fireplace masonry, however, are carried up all the way to the ceiling, leaving unused space boxed in with studs and plaster. The unknown housewright used this space, as shown, with two small cuddies (originally having doors) which are fitted with shelves. The over-mantel effect is most successful. Most of Vermont's corner fireplaces are in Bennington County and may be the work of this unknown man. This easy way of enriching an otherwise bald space is worth copying.

Two early Americans, both scientists, studied chimneys and fireplaces in efforts to better their efficiency. Benjamin Franklin worried about the amount of heat that was wasted by warming the brickwork, as well as going up the chimney. He gave us the Franklin stove, which in effect brings a small open fire right out into the room, its little metal container heating the room, not the brick chimney. These may be bought today, and are excellent for use in bedrooms that cannot have fireplaces. Many such rooms already have a stove-pipe hole, a leftover from times before central heating had been invented. A Franklin stove may be connected to a flue of generous size and make hardly any difference in the draft of the fireplace below.

The other genius was born (1753) in Massachusetts as plain Benjamin Thompson. He was a mathematical prodigy, a wanderer and adventurer, and died in Paris (1814) as Count Rumford of the Holy Roman Empire. His researches resulted in some useful formulae that relate area of fireplace opening to the necessary area of flue and both of these to height of chimney above the fireplace. They are the basis of today's recommendations.

Whether a new chimney and its fireplaces is to be built on existing cellar foundations or not, the first consideration is the width of the fireplace, for chimneys, fireplaces, and mantels all work together. The size of the fireplace opening affects that of the flue which is also related to chimney height. The linecut, Figure 93, shows the various parts in detail according to good modern practise. It should serve as a guide, modified by local conditions. The average living room will be suitably served by a fireplace 36 inches wide. The next larger, 42 inches, is a maximum, and a bedroom fireplace can easily get along with a width of 32 inches, or it may even be as small as 30 inches wide, the minimum.

The size of the ground-floor fireplace determines the dimensions of the ash-pit beneath it in the cellar. The ashpit is such a very great convenience that if construction starts at the cellar floor it ought to be considered essential. It is number 10 in the illustration. The small cast-iron ash dump (number 9) is set in the hearth of the fireplace, fairly close to the back and about in the middle.

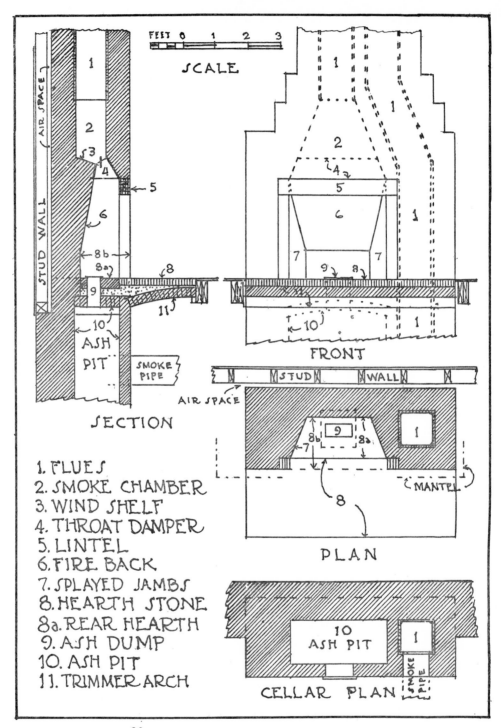

SCALE

SECTION

FRONT

PLAN

CELLAR PLAN

1. FLUES
2. SMOKE CHAMBER
3. WIND SHELF
4. THROAT DAMPER
5. LINTEL
6. FIRE BACK
7. SPLAYED JAMBS
8. HEARTH STONE
8a. REAR HEARTH
9. ASH DUMP
10. ASH PIT
11. TRIMMER ARCH

93 : CONSTRUCTION DETAILS FOR FIREPLACE

Ash dumps are stock articles and are made in various sizes with a pivoted lid that may be operated with the poker or fire shovel. The pivots are off center, so it is self-closing. It is possible to have one in the hearth of a second-floor fireplace, opening into a flue to carry the ashes (*not* a smoke flue) which runs down all the way to the ashpit in the cellar. As there is a possibility of this getting clogged by careless use, like dumping half-burned wood with the ashes, and cleaning of the stoppage would be very difficult, it is usually dispensed with.

Those who are accustomed to using open fires know the value of keeping a bed of ashes on the hearth, beneath the andirons. A new fire on a clean hearth does not burn well. After the first blaze of kindlings even dry wood is reluctant to burn, although it may be a "breakfast fire" of small dry sticks. It may take a week of such short-term fires to provide enough ashes for the fire to burn steadily. Do not let a tidy housewife sweep the fireplace clean after every fire. Those who must have a spotlessly clean hearth had better content themselves with the pitiful show of white birch logs that are never burned, fronted by highly polished brass andirons. That is too much like the colored illustration in a recent magazine that went so far as to show the entire interior of the fireplace recess *painted white*. It is far better to go back to the way of our ancestors and to lay a new fire, after the last smoldering coals have cooled, all ready to light. It will protect the ashes from downdrafts which might blow them out over the hearth, and even the most ardent fire worshipper will approve sweeping such strays back under the waiting logs.

During the work of rebuilding, it is wise to check on the location of the oil-burner smoke pipe. Too often this sheet-metal pipe is set close up under the floor beams, and this is dangerous. If it cannot be set with 18 inches between its top and the bottom of the beams, place a sheet-metal protection about 30 inches wide, half a dozen inches below the beams, to protect them from excessive heat. The opening into the chimney flue that serves the oil burner should have a suitable thimble. The flue should be carried down below this opening and provided with a cast-iron cleanout door at the bottom, of approximately the width of the flue. It is surprising what may be found there when the flue is cleaned! Young starlings, for example, like the heat coming up to the top of the chimney, the fumes overcome them, and they fall down to the pocket below the thimble. The master of the house should also be sure that the ashpit and cleanout doors are wide enough for a shovel to be used when removing ashes. Of course all cleanout doors should have suitable latches so they will stay shut.

Coming upstairs and consulting the details of the line cut, the plan shows a flue from the cellar (1), the fireplace opening with its back (6), and splayed sides (7), as well as the hearth (8). If the house is heated by a coal-burning furnace or boiler, it will require the large flue shown. This should have terra-cotta flue lining, probably the 13 by 13 inch size unless the equally efficient 12-inch circular lining is used. Smoke usually travels in a spiral, slowly if the draft is gentle and faster with a newly kindled fire. In theory that leaves part of a square flue unused. An oil burner, with its forced draft, can get on with a smaller flue—an 8 1/2 by 13 inch one might serve. A fireplace 36 inches wide will almost certainly require the 13 by 13 inch size. If the fireplace is not in the main house, but in a wing or ell, its shorter chimney may require the next size larger for a 36-inch fireplace and certainly would for a 42-inch one, perhaps a 13 by 18 inch rectangular one. The size may be determined by the way the two, or more, flues can be combined, side by side, in the chimney stack. This, in turn, should be built so there is *at least* an inch of air space or asbestos fire-stopping between it and the timbers of walls and floors. With proper flue linings, the stack may be built with four-inch walls, but if that is done, more space, two inches, should be left between the brickwork and wood. If the fireplace is on an end wall, it is better to have its back a full foot thick but still with the space between bricks and wood framing. As stated in the preceding chapter, if the stack is built with flue linings and four-inch walls it should be increased in bulk by using eight-inch walls around the flues from the inside of the attic where it passes through the roof all the way to its top.

The floor of the fireplace, sometimes called "rear hearth," should be on a level with the true hearth, and both of them built level with the finished floor of the room, if the fireplace is to be an authentic Colonial one, in harmony with the house. There are also practical reasons of efficiency and safety for this relationship. In a new fashion, the fireplace is lifted up as much as two feet and has no hearth; or, as a variant, the whole affair, hearth and all, are lifted a considerable distance above the floor. Many of these fireplaces are purely ornamental, lacking flues of any sort, meant only to be looked at. Some are not intended for fireplaces but for grilles, and as such belong in a "rumpus room" rather than a dining or living room. These may be passed over in this book.

The hearth of an "authentic" Colonial fireplace should be level with the floor. It is carried on suitable cement filling (8 a in Figure 93) and in the part within the fireplace recess (8 b) should be of the same brick that is used for the recess. Good hard handmade bricks were available when the old houses were built and these were set flatways for the entire hearth, both within the fireplace recess and in the true hearth (8) in front of the chimney. Modern bricks, however, have to be set on edge, as the beds (which are as perfect in handmade brick as the other four faces) are not fit to be exposed to view. They are either too rough or bear the brickyard's name or initials. In most of the finer houses the outer hearth (8) is not of brick but made of one big slab of marble, soapstone, or slate, at least two inches thick. This outer or true hearth is supported by a brick "trimmer arch" (11). One side of this arch is supported by the wall of the ashpit, the other, which butts against one of the floor timbers, is held in place by a batten nailed to the timber. As a rule, the wooden "center" or form on which the bricks are laid to form this arch, is left in place. The similar center used in building the arched top of the ashpit should be removed when the cement mortar between the bricks has hardened. It should be made with a suitable hole (9) through which the ash dump discharges the ashes from the hearth into the ashpit.

The fireplace recess as shown in Figure 93 has right-angled corners at the front. This is good practise especially if the fireplace and chimney front are of brick. More formal fireplaces have marble "corner posts" here, four inches square in plan and extending from the matching marble hearth to the lintel of the same material. As the usual bricks measure about 8 inches long, 4 inches wide, and about 2 1/4 inches high, these figures will be approximate units for the measurements that are given here, the mortar joints by being thick or thin, giving some leeway. Many old fireplaces that were lined with soapstone or its equivalent had their splayed sides (7) brought out all the way to the front, thus eliminating the right-angled corner. There is no special advantage in this.

Building a fireplace by the old method is strongly recommended. In this the lining of the fireplace recess (if of brick) was made a part of the fabric, as the masonry courses were laid. A modern method is to build a larger recess, then line it with some material other than brick—soapstone, tile, or little briquettes. This is not advised because it is not structurally strong. Another variation is to use firebrick for the entire lining, a material capable of withstanding far higher temperatures than are met with in a wood fire. They are not necessary from that viewpoint. Firebricks are also larger than the so-called "common" bricks, so they cannot be bonded into the fabric properly and their yellowish color is not especially pleasing. The durability of good hard-burned common brick is obvious from fireplaces that have been used for a century and a half with very slight damage to the brick surface. Unfortunately, if the breast as well as the hearth is of brick, a white efflorescence may appear on the surface. If mortar from the joints has accidentally been smeared on exposed masonry it can be removed by washing with dilute hydrochloric (muriatic) acid, which will also remove the efflorescence. After the brickwork and its mortar joints are thoroughly dry, one or two coats of a transparent brick-waterproofing should be brushed on to prevent any further defacement. Very old hearths have had so many applications of soapy water by the housewife that they have acquired a very pleasing dull luster. Some get this effect more quickly by applying floor-wax, or linseed oil, although this may get sticky.

The best way to make sure of correct side splays and slope of the back of the fireplace recess is to construct a wooden form around which the bricks may be laid. The splay and slope are very important and few modern masons can carry the slope up properly without such a form. The rear of the recess should be vertical for five courses of brick before the back slope begins. The location of the slope of the recess is important for heating efficiency as well as good draft. With an opening of 36 inches, the depth of the recess should not be less than 16 inches and 18 inches is a maximum. A 42-inch opening may be made 20 inches deep. The sloping parts of the fireplace affect its ability to throw heat out into the room, for heat is reflected almost like light. Hot air rises, and the more heat reflected down towards the floor, the better. That is another, and practical, reason why the hearth should be at floor level.

The old-time kitchen fireplaces, designed for cooking, are governed by different construction rules. Although the sides were frequently splayed, the entire back was kept vertical, so kettles hung from the crane might be at variable heights above the fireplace according to culinary requirements, as has been previously stated. The lintel was high so the cook could actually get partly inside the recess. To prevent the smoke coming out into the kitchen, the recess was raised above this lintel before the "smoke chamber" began its long taper to the flue.

A fireplace meant for heating had very different proportions. An old one usually draws satisfactorily. The smoke goes up chimney and does not come out into the room unless the logs have been laid too close to the front, due to andirons whose horizontal bars are too long for the fireplace. In building a new fireplace, or making a restoration of an old chimney and fireplace, few modern brickmasons can be trusted to design and build it properly—and they are a very stubborn class of workmen! New work or restoration is an expensive operation, and the owner should insist on the design and text suggestions give in this chapter being followed faithfully. It is in the *upper* portions of the fireplace, quite out of sight, that unwise design may result in a smoky fireplace, a pest instead of the joy that was expected.

The fireplace opening is frequently made too high. A fireplace with an opening 36 inches wide should have a horizontal top or lintel only about 30 inches above the hearth. This is a proportion pleasing to look at and has considerable effect on the size of flue that is required, which, in turn, affects the cost. The lintel may be of stone or marble about four inches thick, and have a bearing on the side walls of the opening of not less than four inches at each end. If it is built of brick, as was frequent in old work, there should be an iron bar about half an inch thick and three inches wide, with the same bearing on the side wall as the stone. On this, the brick may be laid as headers or, more ornamentally, in a flat arch as suggested in the cut. This requires either careful and expensive shaping of each brick or varying thickness of the mortar joints between them. It is very important that this lintel be carried up vertically on the inside of the fireplace at least six inches before the throat damper (4) is bedded on it and at the top of the sloping back. The usual stock damper has a slanting front so the wall of the chimney breast may be increased to eight inches thick at the smoke chamber (2). A curved top instead of a lintel for the fireplace recess does not harmonize with any mantel designs, and should not be used.

Throat dampers come in various patterns. Essentially, there is a cast-iron frame with flanges that bear at least an inch on the masonry, and a long damper, pivoted at its ends, which may be closed or opened either by using a poker or by turning a handle which operates a worm gear and screw. The former is positive, simple, and inexpensive but not easy to get at for adjusting. The gear-and-screw is easy to work, but unless worked until the damper is completely open, or shut, may give trouble with the draft. The poker-operated type is also easier to remove from the frame when the chimney is cleaned.

The smoke chamber and its wind shelf are also important, but, unfortunately, out of sight like the damper. As shown in Figure 93, the front and back walls should be vertical and the side walls tapered up to the flue. According to conditions, these slopes may be symmetrical or not. The best draft, no doubt, is with the flue directly over the middle line of the fireplace, but circumstances may make it necessary to set the flue off center. If height permits, this shift should be made in the flue, not the smoke chamber. The taper, as indicated in the cut, is made by setting each course or layer of bricks a little farther over than the one below, but never more than one inch. Joints should be full and troweled smooth, but no "parging," or plastering over the bricks to make a smooth mortar surface, should be permitted. Parts of such parging, as previously stated, may become detached from the brickwork and hinge over, obstructing the draft, and are very difficult to get at for removal. The wind shelf, however, may have mortar smoothed over its top surface, sloping a little towards the damper. In theory at least, cold drafts pouring down chimney in winter hit the shelf and are deflected into the rapidly rising hot air from the fireplace to join the upward rush of smoke, instead of puffing out into the room. The smoke chamber should, of course, terminate in a sort of shelf about an inch wide to receive the end of the terra-cotta flue lining securely (Items 1 to 2 in the line cut).

The size of the flue, according to most authorities, is based on two factors: the area of the fireplace opening and the height of the chimney above the hearth. This seems sensible. The chimney height is a variable, depending on the number of stories in the house, the slope of the roof, and the location of the chimney due to presence or absence of trees close by, the density of their foliage and branching, as well as the direction of the prevailing winds. There is some question, too, about the *available* area of a flue as something different from the area of its cross section. For example, a circular flue of a given area might give a better draft than one that was a narrow slit of the same number of square inches.

The best guide is experience. The usual two-story house of New England Colonial design which has been satisfactorily served by flues of a certain shape and size leading from conventionally dimensioned fireplaces will be a safe guide under similar conditions. To plan the best flue for a freak fireplace in the middle of an almost flat-roofed Ranch-type house calls for intelligent guesswork. The catalogs of some of the makers of throat dampers contain tables that recommend certain flues for fireplaces of the usual openings. Generally speaking, then, a fireplace that is 36 inches wide and 30 inches high, its smoke chamber etc. following the suggestions of Figure 93, will require either a 13 by 13 inch flue lining, or, under especially good conditions and a chimney of at least 35 feet in height, it might draw successfully with an 8 1/2 by 13 inch flue. If the fireplace is to be 42 inches wide and the height of its opening 30 or 32 inches, the 13 by 13 inch flue lining might serve but the 12 inch circular one would be safer in a tall chimney. That sounds like nonsense, but by one of those odd trade-customs of nomenclature, rectangular flues are described by their nominal *exterior* dimensions and round ones by their nominal *interior* diameter. The 13 by 13 inch lining has walls that are seven-eighths of an inch thick, with round corners. The "effective area" is listed as 99 square inches, but because warm air or hot smoke are supposed to travel in a spiral column there would be a certain amount of skin friction when a fire was being started in a cold chimney. The 12 inch *inside* diameter circular flue, on the contrary, has walls an inch thick (14 inches *outside* diameter), and the "effective area" is given as 113 square inches, which is almost fourteen percent larger as well as being of a more efficient cross section! If the 42 inch-wide fireplace had its height increased by a couple of courses of brick to about 35 inches, it would be safer to use a larger flue. If the fireplace is to be in a one-story ell, wing, or separate small house, the 36 inch-wide fireplace should have about the same size flue as required by the 42 inch one in a two-story house, and so on.

In the previous chapter reference was made to down drafts in the chimney of a salt-box type of house. This house has two chimney stacks, each with three flues. The southerly one includes an 8 1/2 by 13 inch flue (rated at seventy square inches area), serving a fireplace that has an opening 36 inches wide and 30 inches high. It never smokes when a fire is burning in it, but, as previously stated, does suffer from down drafts in cold weather, especially if high winds blow from an easterly direction up the long salt-box roof. The northerly chimney serves two fireplaces, one being 36 inches by 30 inches and the other 42 inches wide and thirty inches high. Both are served by the same sized flues, nominal 12 inch circular ones, with areas of 113 square inches. Neither ever smokes, nor do down drafts occur except on very rare occasions. The round flues were used in the northerly chimney to make the brick laying easier. For the same reason the southerly chimney had rectangular flues on account of the ease of laying the bricks. The 13 inch dimension was common to all three flues, although two of them required 13 by 13 inch flues and the other an 8 1/2 by 13 inch.

Another example may be given, where a costly mistake was made and several hundred dollars wasted in building a fireplace that is seldom used because it often belches smoke out into the room. The fireplace and chimney were properly designed and if they had been built from the plans given the mason there would have been no trouble. Unfortunately, a good many country masons are stubborn, have low opinions of architects, and are apt to be contemptuous of "city theorists." The fireplace serving this single-roomed little hideaway was intended to be its sole source of heat. It was set in the middle of the side wall, partly outside the frame (to save space) and was planned to have an opening 36 inches wide and 30 inches high, with the throat damper set three courses of brick (about 7 1/2 inches) above the lintel of the fireplace opening. The top of the chimney with its 13 by 13 inch flue was planned to be 30 inches above the ridge of the roof. The owner had to be away for several weeks and there was nobody to see that the mason followed orders and drawings. When he returned, the work was completed, according to the way the *mason* thought it should be done. The fireplace opening was made 36 inches high instead of 30, and the flange of the throat damper was used to support the lintel. An 8 1/2 by 13 flue lining had been used—"That's the size I always use" quoth the mason—and the chimney top was only 18 inches above the ridge. In an effort to improve matters, the chimney height was increased by four feet and an eyebrow-like hood of copper, projecting a couple of inches from the chimney breast, was added to reduce the excessively high fireplace opening. These helped a little, but it remains, a costly series of errors. A few years later the same architect designed a tiny studio-cabin of about the same size, using almost the identical dimensions of his *original* plans that the stubborn mason had not followed. The resulting fireplace was eminently satisfactory, never smoking, heating the room adequately. The costly lesson is plain. If the chimney has to be a low one, the flue must be considerably larger than the size given in the tables and the throat damper *must* be set well up above the under side of the lintel.

Modern inventiveness has devised ready-made fireplaces that may be built in without possibility of error by anyone who can lay bricks. They have hollow air chambers which draw in fresh air from outside or from the room, discharging it through registers, in addition to the radiant heat of the open fire itself. They may even carry the heated air through suitable ducts to a room overhead. Made of heavy gauge sheet metal, they will last for quite a while but would be very expensive to rip out when they burned or rusted through and had to be replaced, and of course their durability does not compare with masonry. To those who feel no dislike of a possible twenty-five-year depreciation period and who cannot get an adequate mason, they have some attraction. The "black hole" of the fireplace recess does not appeal to the conservative lovers of the real old fireplaces, however.

The "beloved anachronism" is not cheap, but its addicts are willing to pay the price.

94: STONE TAVERN, ALBURG
Ladies' parlor mantel

[IX]

MANTELS:
CRAFTSMAN'S DELIGHT

THE MANTEL is the only interior feature that is purely decorative. Unhampered by functional limitations, the old housewrights gave free rein to their imaginations and took delight in designing mantels that were in harmony with their surroundings, yet highly individual in their details. The foundation of a mantel design, literally as well as figuratively, is a framework consisting of two upright boards and a horizontal top one, usually with a shelf above it, which surrounds the fireplace recess. Despite this unvarying foundation, craftsmen's ingenuity produced an amazing number of variations on the theme, so it is difficult to treat the subject adequately in a few pages. This Chapter, therefore, omits elaborate examples. It is restricted to those which are simple enough to be reproduced by any reasonably skilful carpenter or amateur. The illustrations are mostly in pairs—a general view with enough of the surroundings to give scale and a large-sized detail picture. From these it is hoped that such a man can get ideas for design as well as suggestions for the use of stock mouldings or modifications thereof made possible by modern machine tools.

In early houses with boarded walls the fireplace recess had merely a sort of "picture-frame" moulding around it. There was no shelf (Fig. 7). The high kitchen fireplace added a shelf. Those in other rooms, in later days when walls were plastered, kept to this type (Fig. 94), using moulded trim not unlike that of the doorways together with further embellishments as the desire for decoration increased among craftsmen and their customers. Development continued with passing years and new forms appeared. The "picture-frame" type was replaced by one that used pilasters of a sort. The mantel shelf, originally a

95: STONE TAVERN, ALBURG
Ladies' parlor mantel detail

board with rounded or moulded edge, became thicker, with a hint of the classic cornice, described in Chapter III, which was abetted by enrichment of the mouldings beneath it. The original plain space beneath these—actually an exposed part of the mantel-frame—became a quasi-frieze, often with a panel of sorts in the middle. The mouldings immediately above the fireplace recess were reminiscent of the architrave. The plainer mantels, like those that are shown in this book, used pilasters with shafts that varied from a flat surface, through paneling, to fluting. Their bases were usually plain blocks, their caps very simple, often formed by the mouldings beneath the mantel shelf breaking out around the slight projection of the shafts.

Up in the extreme northwestern part of Vermont the town of Alburg points down from Canada into Lake Champlain. In the heyday of lake trade a stone tavern was built, and an unknown housewright, perhaps bored a little by the

96: STONE TAVERN, ALBURG
Ballrom mantel

severity of the mason-work, let himself go in designing the interior woodwork. Obviously, he was a man of refined taste, disliking ostentation as well as conservatism. The result was a series of mantels, alike in basic design but varying in their ingenious details. Any fellow craftsman can understand his delight in the result and may feel an urge to share it. Two of the three examples of his work shown here are of the "picture-frame" type. The first, in what may have been the Ladies' Parlor in old days, shows the fireplace trim raised up to the mouldings beneath the shelf (Figs. 94, 95), leaving narrow strips of the mantel frame exposed at the sides of the fireplace recess and a wide plain board at the top. It is a conservative design, entirely in keeping with the purpose of the room. This would not be a difficult mantel for a home craftsman to make, as the effect is entirely dependent on the mouldings. A little searching would result in finding suitable patterns in the local lumber mill. Overall proportion is important.

The second of these mantels is in the adjoining Ballroom and follows the general scheme of the first but is gayer in detail (Figs. 96, 97). The fireplace trim and the shelf group have rope mouldings, which could be made in a screw-cutting lathe. The distinctive feature is the thin strip above the recess trim, jig-sawed out into an unusual and engaging pattern. It is used also in a third mantel, shown in Figure 118. The thin strips should not be over a quarter-inch thick. Rope mouldings may sometimes be bought at a cabinet maker's supply store, usually of hardwood, but this can be painted. Most mantels are painted to match the trim of the room.

If the mantel is at shoulder height and the trim of the fireplace is set close to its recess, an empty space is left that has to be filled. Figure 98 shows one solution of the problem—a thin piece of wood has been set on the mantel frame, its ends sawed out to a graceful shape to join the two sets of mouldings. This is an ingenious way to reduce the length of the shelf, where space is cramped. The cutout will look best if the thickness is about half an inch. In other illlustrations, variants of this scheme are shown.

If the mantel shelf is longer than the width of the frame the thin cutout cannot be used. Instead, as shown in Figure 99, a moulding can be used to fill the gap. In this example it looks like a stock cornice cyma set flatways with its bottom strip cut off. That is one way to modify a stock moulding! Much of the fun

97: STONE TAVERN, ALBURG
Ballroom mantel detail

98: ANGEVINE HOUSE, POULTNEY
Mantel detail, frieze end

to a do-it-yourself man is in discovering ways to change stock mouldings to get a desired effect.

The space between the shelf mouldings and the "picture-frame" is seldom moulded—but why not? Of course, a usual solution for the bare space is to leave it bare. That was what an old craftsman did in the Pettengill House, in which a very small fireplace has almost all the mantel frame exposed to view. With a charming but very narrow mantel trim and graceful mouldings beneath the shelf, it needs no other decoration (Fig. 100). The placing of the narrow mantel trim where it is horizontal is just right. If it had been only a little higher or lower, the resulting change in width of the flat boards would have been disastrous.

Another solution with the space bare is to place a block at each end, the width of the side member of the mantel frame. As shown in Figure 101 the block has a narrow, fine-scaled moulding around it like a tiny picture frame. The treatment under the shelf itself is unusual—a row of short cylinders and a square-edged thin board above them, immediately below it. Due to the thickness

99: LAWRENCE HOUSE, SUNDERLAND
Parlor mantel detail, shelf

100: PETTENGILL HOUSE, GRAFTON
Bedroom mantel detail

of the end blocks, this peculiar but successful decoration has to be broken out around them.

One of the most distinguished mantels of the "picture-frame" variety is in Governor Galusha's house. There does not seem to be another like it in Vermont. The detail is shown in Figure 102. The side pieces of the mantel frame are carried from floor to ceiling where they meet a horizontal top member of equal width, forming an overmantel. There are two intermediate horizontal members, one that is partly exposed at the fireplace opening, the other being almost altogether behind the mantel and its mouldings. The space in between is filled by four flat panels, each with a narrow moulding around its edges. In the overmantel the legendary "wandering foreigner" painted, freehand, a flower piece in subdued colors. However, it is the ornamental work beneath the mantel shelf that arouses a craftsman's enthusiasm, for it is so very striking, yet not hard to make.

Fundamentally it consists of a board about half an inch thick, part of which

101: BEN HULETT HOUSE, SHAFTSBURY
Bedroom mantel detail

102: GOVERNOR GALUSHA HOUSE,
SHAFTSBURY
Bedroom mantel and overmantel

lies behind the sensitively curved moulding that stiffens the mantel shelf. The rest of this board is partly cut away to a quarter-inch thickness, leaving a row of dentils in relief, the original surface showing between them and the cove. Beneath the dentils is a row of little diamonds, incised perhaps a sixteenth of an inch, but their square edges still catching the light after nearly a hundred and fifty years of painting and repainting. As the focus for a room it is peerless, yet there is nothing about it that could not be made in a home workshop if the enthusiastic craftsman would use carver's tools for the fine work on that quarter-inch-thick strip. Of course, an artist friend who would provide a landscape painting would help!

The Farrar-Mansur House in Weston is a fine example of an amateur restoration of a lovely old building, now the Community Center. A group of enthusiasts, while doing it, rescued the mantel shown in Figures 103 and 104 from the wreckage of another house. It may be more elaborate than is required in that simple building but it has points worthy of study if one were making a

103: FARRAR-MANSUR HOUSE, WESTON
Bedroom mantel detail

plainer variant of the design. The mantel mouldings could be greatly simplified. If the shelf were built up of two boards that were not of the same thickness, one perhaps 7/8-inch thick and the lower 5/8, their edges might be left square, or that of the top board only, slightly rounded. In the quasi-frieze, all the reeded squares might be omitted with profit, except those on the end blocks. The little reeded uprights that mark the ends are worth keeping and the dentil treatment is admirable. The very simple fireplace trim is good; rather pleasant after the usual "door-casing" sort. There are several other excellent mantels in the building, not illustrated here, but well worth seeing by the lover of oldtime craftsmanship.

In many cases an enrichment of the mantel may be made by changing the method of supporting the shelf. Figures 105 and 106 show pilasters from the floor level up to it which reduce the "picture-frame" trim. This mantel may be the ultimate in plainness, but how well it harmonizes with the simplicity of the room!

Figures 107 and 108 show a parlor mantel. Many of its mouldings are of shapes that cannot be found in stock material. Their elliptical section is import-

104: FARRAR-MANSUR HOUSE, WESTON
Bedroom mantel and overmantel

ant to the effect, especially that of the edge of the mantel shelf. The design
depends on its proportions and contrasts between mouldings and plain flat
surfaces, but it would be hard to copy.

The slender pilasters, their bases a continuation of the low baseboard of the
room, run up to the shelf. Their caps are made of the shelf's bed mould, broken
out around the unadorned upper part or necking of the pilasters. The flutes,
with their tiny grooves between them, are essential to the design. So is the flat
block in the middle of the "frieze." The effect is very pleasing and most suitable
to a simple room. It is of the essence of New England and would be a challenge
to a home craftsman.

105: PETTENGILL HOUSE, GRAFTON
West wall, child's bedroom

106: PETTENGILL HOUSE, GRAFTON
Child's bedroom mantel detail

Figures 109 and 110 show a mantel designed by a New York man. If we compare the Brick House and Hard Tavern mantels, it is plain that both are essentially of the same scheme, but with strikingly different proportions. In Brick House the mantel frame is so much wider that it receives the projection of the narrow shelf. The pilasters are set in the middle of the uprights of the frame, and are wider than those in the Hard Tavern design, with *four* flutes, two being quite small, the outer pair about as wide as those of the Hard Tavern pilasters. These flutes are apparently cut out of the shaft, while in the Hard Tavern example they seem to be separate pieces inserted in a recess. With the exception of the moulding directly under the shelf, suitable stock mouldings could be used in a copy. A close inspection of the illustrations and their captions will show that two mantels are represented. The only apparent difference is in the treatment of the edge of the shelf. In the West Room this has a little S-section moulding applied at the top, while the other mantel keeps its square edge, with two very small half-rounds applied to smooth off the square; a hint to the

107: HARD TAVERN, EAST ARLINGTON
Southwest parlor mantel

108: HARD TAVERN, EAST ARLINGTON
Southwest parlor mantel detail

home craftsman and an example of the obvious delight the old handworkers took in their trade.

When old houses are torn down some of their elements may be too good to be taken to the town dump. In one such case the mantel shown in Figures 111 and 112 was salvaged from the usual ignominious fate. Placed in a room with unpainted trim, the heavy coats of old paint were removed from the mantel, and on the middle panel of the frieze an old painting was found! There seems to have been a fashion for this sort of thing in Victorian days when young ladies

109: BRICK HOUSE, ARLINGTON
East bedroom mantel

110: BRICK HOUSE, ARLINGTON
East bedroom mantel detail

"fainted in coils." The general scheme is a conventional one of its type, but interest as well as enrichment is added by fluting the pilasters (which against all Classic tradition have an entasis or taper) and by the groups of flutes in the flat member under the cornice. Also, the entablature, if we can call it that, is broken out from the general projection of the shelf. While the mouldings are excellent, there is no reason why modern stock mouldings of similar proportions should not be used in a new mantel.

A variation from the type shown in the preceding illustrations and one easier

111: CARPENTER HOUSE, FAIR HAVEN
Living room mantel

to make is shown in Figures 113 and 114. Here the pilasters are paneled and stock mouldings could be used, for the profile of the moulding is of less importance in this type of mantel than the scale and size of the moulding strip. The strongly marked horizontal lines of the shelf and the fireplace trim, accompanied by the breaking out of the extension of the pilasters, add a pleasing serenity to the design and the shadows cast by the pilasters save it from monotony. The groups of reeding give the needed enrichment, a touch of individuality that is very welcome. Probably stop-cut flutes, a little wider than the reeds, might make a suitable substitute if the mantel were to be copied. They would be easy to make with a sharp carpenter's gouge if it were ground with a long bevel, or a

112: CARPENTER HOUSE, FAIR HAVEN
Living room mantel detail

113: KETCHAM HOUSE, WALLINGFORD
Dining room mantel detail

wood-carver's gouge with a deep sweep would be even better. The effect of the entire design is helped by the useful cuddy with its panelled door, and the shelves inside are a great convenience for storing dishes.

Ebenezer Robinson's "new mantels," to which reference has already been made, are all four of practically the same design, varying only in their details, and it is likely that these pleasing and ingenious variations are his own. Figure 115 and Figure 116 show the mantel in his Northwest Parlor, with its overmantel framed by reeded pilasters. The detail under the shelf is peculiar. Apparently a strip of the curious scallopy dentils has been set in *flatways* just under the bed mould above. The overmantel in the bedroom is framed with

114: KETCHAM HOUSE, WALLINGFORD
East wall of dining room

plain boards (Fig. 9). The mantel pilasters are reeded instead of paneled, with an odd little sunburst carved just above the pilaster cap—a "craftsman's delight"! This is shown in Figure 117.

The "scallopy dentils" in the Robinson mantel were jigsawed out of thin wood. This manner of decoration is not unusual. It is seen in one of the mantels in Alburg's Stone Tavern (Fig. 118), where a strip of thin wood has been cut to a shape reminiscent of the Classic egg-and-dart. The conventional panel in the middle of the frieze has an oval hole cut in it through which the plain frieze shows, its oval shape echoing the "eggs" of the little strip above. There is something artless about this treatment—the sophisticated Massachusetts craftsmen

115: ROBINSON HOUSE, SOUTH READING
Northwest parlor mantel detail

116: ROBINSON HOUSE, SOUTH READING
Parlor mantel and overmantel

117: ROBINSON HOUSE, SOUTH READING
Northwest bedroom mantel detail

118: STONE TAVERN, ALBURG
Pilaster type mantel detail

might have deemed it unworthy of their skill, but a modern do-it-yourself man need not be afraid to use it.

A plain mantel, even of the type that uses pilasters, may seem too severe if these pilasters have neither paneling nor flutes. The short space between the cap and necking is often used for a simple "spot," either an incised sunburst as in the Robinson mantel (Fig. 117) or an applied flower (Fig. 119), which was used in the Sargent-Leach design. A little touch like this may go a long way to transform a stodgy design to an imaginative one.

If the mouldings of the mantel shelf (those on its edge and the group immediately beneath it) are too small in scale, three panels in the length of the frieze and a little diamond made of mouldings applied to the upper part of the pilaster

119: SARGENT-LEACH HOUSE, PAWLET
Southeast parlor mantel detail

120: KETCHAM HOUSE, WALLINGFORD
Parlor mantel detail

will do much to cure the defect (Fig. 120) and improve the entire composition.

In old times when good clear pine was used for mantel building and was not as expensive as it is today, a smoothly planed board, such as is used for a mantel shelf, was about an inch thick and in many cases the housewrights thought that this was enough. They even made it appear thinner by applying mouldings to it, as shown in many of the illustrations. Later master builders tried various devices to overcome this defect in scale. The unknown man who made the mantel in the Kellog parlor (Fig. 121) had what he thought was a better idea than using two boards, the lower one a trifle narrower, as shown in previous examples. His device is very decorative, but must have taken him a great deal of time to make, for small upright reeds, set just a little apart, had to be cut to

121: KELLOG HOUSE, BENSON
Rear parlor mantel detail

122: RICH TAVERN, EAST MONTPELIER
Ballroom mantel detail

length and fastened in place between the mouldings. These seem to be made of narrow half-round moulding. Perhaps they were made by a reeding plane on a thin board, but successive coats of paint applied during many decades hides any joints. The effect is pleasing and adds richness to a rather unimportant division of the mantel.

Another way of making a thicker-appearing shelf was used in the ballroom of the Rich Tavern (Fig. 122). The upper part of the cornice seems to be boxed, with a cove moulding at its top, while the projection is enough to avoid a too-thin appearance. The effect of solidity is heightened by the treatment of the mouldings just above the frieze. These include a prominent dentil course, an approximation of true classic form. These might be made by gluing or bradding

123: MUNRO-HAWKINS HOUSE,
SHAFTSBURY
Southwest parlor mantel detail

half-round mouldings on a thin board, spacing them widely, after which a
router bit of the appropriate diameter, used in a drill press, could cut out the
lower part of the board. Inspection of the illustration will make this clear. It
is a very unusual treatment, and well worth repeating.

True classical dentils are hardly ever used in simple mantels and the large
and richly decorated ones are not within the scope of this book. However, the
men who made the simple village and farmhouse mantels realized the importance
of something akin to dentils, and with their good taste and ingenuity made many
useful variants of the plain classic form. One of these is shown in Figure 123.
Whether this was devised by the master carpenter who worked with Joshua
Munro or came from a contemporary book is unimportant. The picture shows
the classical form, but this is enriched by boring little holes over each gap between dentils, greatly enhancing the decorative effect. Still other variants
are to be found in other mantels of this handsome old farmhouse, which is still

124: EDWARD CONGDON HOUSE, CLARENDON
Northeast parlor mantel detail

standing, little changed from its original condition, alongside a busy highway. One of them (Fig. 75) shows a so-called Greek fret in place of the conventional dentil course, of a taller form than the Classical type.

Another example of the Greek fret motif is on the parlor mantel of the Edward Congdon House in Clarendon (Fig. 124) and is of the true classical proportion but with little holes bored in its horizontal parts. The raised central panel in the frieze has its original egg-and-bead moulding at top and bottom, with a modern replacement of the vertical member of its frame.

Figure 125 shows a modern mantel that follows the old style. It is the product of the joint work of the clergyman-owner of the old house and an intelligent country carpenter, both men well versed in the old traditions. The house was built about 1830, but its old fireplaces and mantels had been removed; the illustration shows reconstruction. The design of the mantel is said to have been derived from the entrance doorway of the house, which is quite like the one

125: EDWARDS HOUSE, ARLINGTON
Modern mantel in study

shown in Figure 43—certainly an unexpected inspiration for a mantel! Possibly other modern restorers may similarly find suggestions for various details in pictures in this book which are intended to illustrate different features. This mantel is an example of the success that may be attained by craftsmen who appreciate and understand good proportions and suitable scale. Stock materials were used, and although all the work was done by hand, the cost was less than that of a quantity-produced machine-made "stock" mantel. Also, the design was better.

Most of the illustrations herein show *painted* woodwork for all the interior trim and details; those with "natural" wood finish are mostly of very old buildings. Persons who prefer this should consider its effect, versus a painted finish (regardless of color), and also should bear in mind the difference between the old, perfectly "clear" wood and the modern preference for "knotty pine" which is easier to get as well as cheaper than the clear. A simple mantel must depend on the play of light and shade on the curved surfaces of its mouldings which will display their beauty better if they are painted, preferably in light tones. Natural finishes are described in Chapter VI, and may darken considerably with age if they have no protective, washable, varnished surface. This darkening is unavoidable. If the "natural" wood be knotty pine, the dark spots and lines in knots and grain may give unexpected emphases and almost certainly fine details of mouldings become less definite with age. This is not true of painted wood.

Figure 126 shows an architect-designed mantel, by no means a copy of an old one, but retaining much of the feeling of old work. The room is fairly large, low-ceilinged, and with exposed hewn beams. The walls are boarded, full height, with very old pine boards, some of them unusually wide, many of them with tight knots. They were found in an old barn, stacked away in a haymow, in the shape of heavy unplaned planks, probably intended for replacement flooring, as they belonged to the time when knotty pine was considered fit only for rough use. Luckily, a local factory had a very large band saw with which these planks were resawed; when they had been run through a planer, the finished thickness was 7/8 inch, quite enough for the purpose. Blind-nailing was impossible for such wide material, so they were secured to the framing of the walls with eight-penny wire casing nails which have very small heads. These were sunk below the surface.

126: H. W. CONGDON HOUSE, ARLINGTON
Modern mantel in studio

The finish used was the kerosene-vehicle type described in Chapter VI, without any further treatment such as varnish. The hewn beams, of red oak, were only slightly seasoned, and the color of their new wood made a most unpleasant contrast with the freshly sawed old pine boards. The two colors were brought in harmony, to almost the same tint, by the stain, and with the passing of more than thirty years both woods have darkened considerably.

The entire chimney breast, front and sides, is ceiled with flush paneling, the only applied ornament being the 3/8-inch-thick pine board at the top. Part of this is jigsawed into four arches. The mantel shelf is carried by the stock mouldings. Perhaps this description and the picture may encourage some home craftsman to "go and do likewise." To be the originator of such an important part of the home, and even more, to make it with one's own hands, gives lasting satisfaction. The fireplace and its mantel can be more than the architectural focus of the room in which it stands, probably the family gathering place. It may be also the spiritual focus of family life. If the structure remains only an ornament, this feature is neglected, for the fire on the hearth has a hidden value far above physical warmth. There is a poem which emphasizes this:

> "The hearth am I, the deep heart of the dwelling,
> A place for quiet mirth and storytelling. . . ."

[X]

GOOD WOOD TO BURN

THERE are plenty of people who know all about fireplace fuel, where to get it, how to choose it. This Chapter is not for them. But there are also those who lack that knowledge, who have become accustomed to press a button to set an oil burner roaring, controlled by thermostats and working through skilfully arranged pipes and radiators. This information is addressed to them.

Back in 1916 a young man found himself commanding a company of a National Guard regiment in a large city. He was worried by his non-commissioned officers' ignorance of outdoor life, so obtained permission to take four of them on a two-week practice march in the Green Mountains of Vermont "for educational purposes." On the second afternoon of their trip through pathless wilderness a heavy rain started as they were making camp. It had already been demonstrated that he would have to be leader, cook, and KP for his willing but ignorant men to whom compass, axe, and frying pan were strange new things. He cut and split two neat little piles of wood while they gathered brittle dead branches and birchbark. He started his fire, hovering over the growing blaze in the downpour, and called "Sergeant, bring me some of that softwood, *quick!*" A man jumped to the woodpiles and stayed there, fumbling and fumbling. "Hop to it!" snarled the officer, "What's the matter?" The sergeant rushed over with three pieces of split *maple,* thumbing their edges. "These are the softest pieces I can find, Sir," said he.

Those who do not see the point of the story the first time they read it need this chapter.

A hundred years ago, rows of suburban homes were built, each with open fireplaces on two floors as well as a hot-air-heater in the cellar. The local "yard" in the suburbs, and even some in the cities, advertised "Coal, Wood & Ice" as a matter of course. Times changed, and now they are changing again. The speculative builder includes a fireplace in the living room and makes it a selling point in his prospectus. To be sure, good wood to burn in it is a costly luxury in Suburbia, so the fireplace is often unused. It may have a few decorative white birch logs on the polished andirons, a souvenir of a trip to Vermont when the family car paused at a roadside stand and Father bought them, neatly tied in a bundle, six pretty little logs for *only* ninety cents!

Those who live in new and growing suburbs, if alert, may find real bargains in wood. Perhaps a new development has a lot of unwanted trees. The contractor may be glad to find a customer for those he has to dispose of, somehow. Even in the older places, there may be a destructive storm and the Village Fathers who must remove the wreckage will welcome inquiries. But it is only those who know something about wood who will profit by such opportunities.

People who have homes in the country are better off. Even with the rapid spread of rural electrification a good many farmers still burn wood in the kitchen stove. It is a cheap fuel for them because most farms have a wood lot. Each winter, when there is little other farmwork to do, the men go out to it and get a year's supply from storm-damaged and cull trees. Many of them have sugar houses, which burn a lot of cordwood. Such farmers are a good source of fireplace fuel if there is no one who makes a business of cutting it for sale. The city man with "a little place in the country" is lucky if he has his own wood lot. It does not need a great deal of wood to supply two or three fireplaces, even for a year-round home. Half a cord per fireplace may be enough.

A good fireplace deserves good wood, the sort that will burn sweetly, yet give out heat. Some kinds, like white birch, which is so pretty in the readied fireplace, burn with little heat and leave a residue of useless charcoal instead of the fine white ashes that are so useful in the garden. Others, like wild cherry, are given to small but violent explosions that shoot out sparks or hot coals, or burn with a smoky red flame and lack the glowing coals needed for heat. The pines and other conifers have that fault, too. Dry spruce burns fast, but snaps like a miniature artillery engagement.

Unquestionably, hardwoods are the best fuel, and apparently the heavier the wood the more heat it gives. Compare the light and inefficient white birch with its heavy cousin, yellow birch, which is a good fuel. Applewood is a luxury wood, not to be had unless there is a worthless, abandoned orchard whose owner wants to get rid of it. You will not find a quieter burning wood or one with a sweeter fragrance. Next in desirability is hard maple—rock maple, sugar maple—and, as this is a self-sown weed tree in many old pastures, it can be had without cutting down a profitable sugarbush. It is easy to work up, for it splits easily. It burns to clean white ashes readily and slowly with a minimum of smoke and a delicate fragrance. Hickory is its equal but is scarce in some parts of the country except in the allied species, "pig-nut," of little use except for fuel. Beech is in the same class and a purchase of mixed hardwoods consisting of these three is a good buy. They give out plenty of heat.

The oaks, like wild cherry, are given to pyrotechnics and are not desirable for open fires. Ash is much better than the oaks. Now that we are afflicted with the Dutch Elm disease many a fine wine-glass or white elm has to be taken down and an alert person can get free wood in consequence. But there is a catch in it. The wood has to be burned before the following spring, if cut in early autumn. The danger is in the bark where the beetle grubs lurk and unless this can be removed and promptly burned, the trunks are of little use until they have had a chance to dry out. The grain of the wood is so felted together that it is very, very hard to split until perfectly dry. The limbs, however, may be used without splitting if not over six inches through. Being rather green, if autumn-cut, they are hard to kindle but, when they once get going in the fireplace, form a bed of hot coals that ignite the replenishment logs. The wood burns like anthracite coal, with small flames and intense heat. The coals do not go out, but keep glowing to fine white ashes. To some, the odor of white-elm smoke is very unpleasant. Oddly enough, others find it equally agreeable. The red elm, not as common as the white, is not used as a shade tree for streets and, it is said, is not so apt to be attacked by the beetle. Country boys call it "slippery elm" and like to peel and chew the inner bark to soothe throat irritations. It splits more easily than the white elm, burns as efficiently, and the smoke has a delicious aromatic fragrance. Basswood and the various poplars are to be avoided, for they are practically fireproof unless very dry and when burning give off little heat.

Usually mixed hardwood is more readily obtained than any specific varieties, for few of the sellers know or care much about open fires. Like everything else, the price has gone up. Wood at $4.50 a cord is like the legendary anthracite coal at $ 9 a ton. Wood is, or should be, sold by the cord of 1,728 cubic feet as measured in a pile that is four feet high and eight feet long, the logs in four foot lengths. To avoid the costly time needed to pile wood for measurement, it is often sold by the "load." It is a matter of simple arithmetic to figure the cubic capacity of a truck body, but if the logs are a bit carelessly thrown in or are somewhat crooked, one pays a good price for several cubic feet of air! Even piling in measured cords can be done from different viewpoints! The buyer's or the seller's. The "running cord," a fractional part of a true cord, the logs sawed to the requested lengths, is also apt to favor the seller. Another favorite way of selling wood is in logs of random length. Any measurement of such a load is pure guesswork, and the guess can hardly be expected to be in the buyer's favor. It should be obvious that a true cord of four-foot lengths will be less after it is sawed to the size wanted and split. That is a legitimate shrinkage.

Newly cut (green) wood is always cheaper than dry, because of the quick turnover. It is wise to buy ahead, purchasing green wood, which is so much easier and quicker to split when dry, and letting it dry outdoors on your place during the summer. If cut in the winter of one year, split in early spring, and piled outdoors until the autumn, it should be good fuel for the second winter. Green wood is not an economical fuel. Much of the heat is used in boiling out the sap. The resulting smoke carries a lot of "creosote" into the flue and more frequent flue-cleaning is required.

It pays to have the wood that has been delivered to one's place cut to the desired lengths by a neighbor who has a "saw rigging." This is a circular saw mounted on the back of an elderly automobile and powered by its engine. It has a swinging rack on which the four-foot logs are placed and cut by pushing the rack towards the saw. The custom sawyer will need instruction and watching. He is used to sawing stove wood which is only twelve inches long, much too short for fireplace use. Four-foot cordwood sawed "twice in three," if carefully done, gives sixteen-inch lengths that are admirable for most fireplaces. Twenty-four-inch wood is right for a larger one. If the wood is delivered in random lengths it will take some judgment on the part of the sawyer to approximate the desired lengths with a minimum of "overs" or useless "shorts."

If sixteen inches is the desirable length, longer pieces are usuable even in a thirty-six-inch fireplace, and merely a nuisance when piling the wood neatly in the woodshed. It is a mistake both from the viewpoint of economy and comfort to use logs that are too long in a fireplace. A disgusted Indian guide said, "White man make big fire, stay long way off, need long-handled fry pan. Injun make little fire, can squat and cook over it."

Next comes splitting the sawed lengths. If you have the time and the skill, or are willing to learn, make a double saving and do your own splitting. It takes a lot of knack to hit the same place twice with an axe. Sinking a long putt takes skill, too. Golf is learned at considerable expense from a professional. Axemanship can be learned from your hired help, but meanwhile he is splitting your wood! The unaccustomed work may take off that soft roll around the waist but the resulting appetite will put it back again. Splitting wood really needs more skill than strength, although it is undeniably hard work if there are many knotty logs. Some green wood splits more easily than dry, so do not wait too long after the cordwood has been sawed into the shorter lengths before splitting. White elm splits best, however, when very dry.

Using the right tools will ease the work. While a razor-sharp axe is best for chopping, a duller one is preferable for splitting. A five-pound axe is thin with a broad edge and, if sharp, cuts the fibres where a duller one splits by wedging them apart. A more useful tool is a "splitting maul." This weighs about eight pounds, is wedge-shaped, nearly three times as thick at the helve as an axe, and has a narrow, rather blunt edge. Muscle is needed to swing the greater weight, but usually one mighty blow will split a reluctant log that would need several from an axe.

If the wood is knotty, steel wedges are used after axe or maul has made an opening cut. These are driven home by repeated blows of the butt end of the splitting maul. They may have to be shifted as the log opens up. A good deal depends on knowing where to place the opening crack. This is learned from experience. Like golf, only a little may be learned from books. The rest comes from instruction and much practise. Some people get as much pleasure from placing an axe blow in exactly the right place with just the right force as they do from a good drive straight down the fairway. Good axemanship has the additional attraction of being useful!

Whoever splits the wood, it is desirable to have the right sizes. Big chunks are good for slow-burning backlogs, or a fire that is to smoulder all day; small pieces for kindling and to make a quick, hot fire at breakfast time on a chilly morning; middle-sized pieces should be in the majority, an average size for an average fire. A few round, unsplit logs are useful—up to six inches diameter for backlogs and some of smaller size for foresticks. Thrifty souls can use a lot of the small branches usually piled and burned as waste. This sort of fuel is gathered by European peasants in their lord's forest and bound into faggots. When dry they make a quick, very hot fire, mighty welcome when you come in from snowshoeing through a blinding snowstorm. These small branches make good kindling, too, but usually they burn so fast and so completely that they make hardly any coals. Indians call them "squaw wood" and campers use them for brief, quick fires. Since these small pieces should be laid with both ends on the andirons they should be of the same length as the other wood. In a fireplace with the usual 36 inch opening the most useful length for firewood, whether large or small in diameter, is 18 inches, which does not work out well if cordwood logs are to be cut up for the fireplace. By placing the andirons a little closer together, the 16 length can be used, which permits the four-foot log to be cut "twice in three" as the woodsmen say. A really big fireplace, say 42 inches wide, could use the more extravagant 24 inch logs, each half of a cordwood one, but it is well to remember that too big a fire may throw out too much heat for comfort.

Piling wood takes some skill. If the ground is uneven, use some poles lengthways of the pile, keeping the front and rear ones level with one another from front to back. This keeps the fuel off the damp ground. Stability of the pile is essential, whether it be a temporary one outdoors, or the supply in the woodshed. It is no laughing matter to have a pile of wood fall on a person. The outdoor woodpile need not have its logs as tightly packed together as the inside one. Plenty of air holes will let the wind blow through and dry out the green wood, but the pile *must* be stable. The trick is to keep the successive rows level. If there are a couple of logs that are bigger at one end than at the other, let the big ends alternate, back and front, as the layers build up. In the woodshed the successive piles can be in contact, but the outdoor ones should have plenty of air space between, to hasten the drying. The walls of the woodshed will support the ends of the piles, but the outdoor ones must have end supports of some sort. The usual one is a post driven in the ground at each end, well braced against the push of the wood. Another way is to "cob house" both ends of the woodpile. This means that the ends of each layer should be of carefully chosen pieces of split wood with flat surfaces—for greater stability—set alternately parallel and at right angles to the length of the row. The name comes from the little square towers country children build with corncobs.

If the outdoor woodpiles are to remain there for over six months, protect the top layers from autumn rains and early snow storms with a covering of boards. When the time comes to fill the woodshed, drying should be complete. Good wood should be really dry to make a cheery fire.

Basil Davenport wrote recently that "building a fire is one of the oldest and easiest of arts." It is old enough to have been completely forgotten by many people in this Machine Age, but easy to those who know how. There are some, lacking a sporting spirit, who keep a small block of porous cement, cast on the end of an iron rod, soaking in a decorative brass pot of kerosene. This malodorous, dripping thing is lighted and put under the logs which shortly burst into flame, perhaps, from the heat of indignation. The contrivance gains a specious respectability by being called a "Cape Cod firelighter." Others build a substructure of packing-box wood on the andirons and top this with honest hardwood. It is very good kindling, but is apt to throw out a barrage of sparks. Also, wooden packing boxes are not common nowadays—corrugated cardboard cartons have taken their place.

One of the ways to build an open fire has at least two virtues: it works and it uses up otherwise worthless old newspapers and the paraffin toppings of last summer's jellies. For its success it needs a good bed of ashes, *not* a heretically clean-swept fireplace (Fig. 127). At the rear, lay a good-sized backlog on the andirons. It may be round, unsplit wood which is slow burning and helps to throw the new fire's heat out into the room. Against it and between the andirons thrust the first of three crumpled balls of newspaper, its core about a third of a wax topping broken in bits. The ball should be well crumpled up, for folded paper does not burn freely. When the space against the backlog and between the andirons is filled with these balls, place the forestick, preferably a thin

127: FOUR STAGES IN LAYING AN OPEN FIRE

unsplit log, and take care that this is not too far out, or when the fire is lighted smoke will come out into the room. Many andirons have a spur near the upright front member, to hold the forestick in its proper position. Make sure that the andirons are of the right length to suit the fireplace depth. Some old fireplaces are very shallow and need short andirons, or they will surely smoke, and it will not be the chimney's fault.

Fill the space between forestick and backlog with rather finely split *dry* wood of a length to rest on the andirons. These pieces will be irregular enough to allow the flames from the paper to run up between them. Lay these sticks with the split side down and the bark side up. Then make a second layer in the same way, the front piece of wood in the crack back of the forestick. Then light the paper. With plenty of ashes beneath the fire, hot, glowing coals will form and help the upper layer to ignite. Many people are too stingy with wood. An open fire is sociable, and lonesome pieces of wood may expire for lack of companionship. Of course, the other extreme, a terrific blaze, may set the chimney on fire.

Keep the fire "picked up." That is, when unburned ends or coals fall outside the andirons, use the tongs, pick them up and put them in convenient gaps. If the wood is a bit on the green side and reluctant to burn, a wisely directed shove with the foot will bring the pieces closer together and encourage combustion. One of the many charms of an open fire is the "fixing" that everyone wants to do. Each of us cherishes a secret belief that we can do the right thing to it better than our neighbor. Too much fussing is no help—but it is a lot of fun. Charles Dudley Warner wrote "To poke a fire gives more solid enjoyment than almost anything else in the world. The crowning virtue in a man is to let his wife poke the fire. . . . If a wood fire is a luxury, it is cheaper than many in which we indulge without thought, and cheaper than the visits of a doctor, made necessary by the want of ventilation in the house."

THE REWARD

THE REWARD

THE MASTER of the house comes back after a walk in the woods. He looks at the maple-shaded building which was old when his grandfather was a boy, glorified by the late afternoon light. His house. Or is it? He bought it, he repaired the rotting eaves and replaced the handsome doorway and three mantels that someone had sold to antique dealers, but is it truly *his?* Has that serene old dwelling, rich with untold tales of men and women long dead, possessed *him?* Never mind. It's a happy place now. He remembers the pleasure he has had in restoring, replacing, even creating new beauties after much reflection. It is akin to his long-forgotten childhood days of "playing house." But this is different. It is not pretense, but reality.

He stops and looks about him, thinking of those who loved the place in other days, thinking, too, of the misty future. Until now he and his family have been wanderers, living in rented dwellings; moving, perhaps, from city to city, suburb to suburb, never able to take root. Here, where his careful planning has guided his handiwork, is home. That is not a name to be lightly spoken. Money may take care of material, practical, needs. Only a home can provide the precious spiritual gifts, so hard to define but essential to true happiness. Breathing deeply of the clean, sweet air, he smiles—contented and very thankful.

Truly, the heart *does* have its radiance!

GLOSSARY

architrave, the bottom group of mouldings in an entablature, *q.v.*

balusters, upright supports of a stair rail resting on the step or floor. See *banister*, *spindle*.

balustrade, a row of balusters.

banister, a corruption of baluster.

beam, a horizontal framing timber usually supporting a floor.

blinds, door-like closures for a window, containing louvers, *q.v.*, which may be fixed or movable and which protect the room from light but permit the free passage of air. See *shutters*.

board, a piece of sawed lumber about an inch thick. See *plank*.

cames, lead strips of H-shaped section that connect pieces of glass, straight or curved, used in fan lights or side lights.

capital, the ornamental top of a column or pilaster. The diminutive form is "cap."

carriage beam, a sloping timber that carries the steps of a staircase.

casings, the trim of flat or moulded boards that surround door and window openings.

ceiled, covered with wide boards set vertically. Sometimes the edges of the boards are moulded. Differs from wainscot, which is paneled.

chair rail, a horizontal strip of wood, usually with a simple moulded cap, set at a height suitable to protect the plastered wall from damage by chair backs. An inexpensive substitute for a low wainscot which would serve the same purpose. It may be the continuation of the window sills.

column, a round or half-round pillar used for support or ornament. The diminutive form is "colonnette."

corbel, a bracket, usually of stone.

cornice, the upper group of mouldings in an entablature, *q.v.*, or the group of mouldings crowning a mantel or some other feature, or decoarting the junction of wall and ceiling.

dentils, small blocks set in a row, ornamenting a cornice.

dry wall, a stone well laid up without mortar.

eave, generally used in the plural. The projection of the lower part of the roof beyond the vertical wall of the house.

ell, an appendage of the main building, its axis or length at right angles to that of the house. See *wing*.

entablature, a group of horizontal moudings carried by columns or pilasters of which the lower group (architrave) is separated from the upper (cornice) by the flat frieze, which is often ornamented.

fan light, a fan-shaped or semicircular window, usually over a door.

fenestration, the orderly and planned arrangement of window and door openings considered as decoration in an architectural composition.

fish tail, a wood carver's term for a short gouge cut ending at a stop-cut, *q.v.*, of the same groove section.

flashing, sheet metal used in valleys of a roof, or where a roof slope meets a vertical wall, or in similar places to waterproof a junction.

flute, or *fluting*, decoration of a column or pilaster by vertical grooves. The opposite of reeding, *q.v.*

frame, framed house, as used in this book, one built in the old-fashioned way with a frame of heavy timbers that support the floor beams, so interior partitions carry no floor load as they do in modern construction.

frieze, the flat middle part of an entablature separating the architrave from the cornice. It may be plain or decorated.

gable roof, one in which the roof slope extends from the eaves to the ridge or top. Eaves and ridge are horizontal as seen from the front; the end view shows the roof slopes of front and back of the building forming a triangular termination of the end wall. This is the gable.

gambrel roof, one in which the roof slope is steep for a distance above the eaves and changes abruptly, part way up, to a flatter pitch which is continued to the ridge. The junction of the two pitches is called the curb.

girder, a heavy timber that carries floor beams.

handrail, the top member of the protecting balustrade of a staircase.

hipped roof, a pyramidal roof in which the horizontal eaves are carried around all four sides of the house; the roof slopes starting from them at the same pitch meet in a short ridge. The junctions of the roof slopes are called hips and the framing timbers beneath them are hip rafters.

lintel, the horizontal member of a door or window opening. It may be of wood or of stone. This term is used similarly in a fireplace opening.

louvers, thin strips of wood set horizontally (as in blinds) to admit air and some light.

modillion, an ornamental bracket, used in a row to decorate a cornice.

mortise and tenon joint, one in which a rectangular cavity (mortise) is cut in a girder or similar timber, and a tongue (tenon) formed on the beam which fits tightly into the mortise. The joint is sometimes made more secure by being pinned with a wooden peg (see *trunnel*).

muntins, narrow wood strips that divide a window sash and support the glass panes.

newel, a sturdy post to which the handrail of a staircase is secured.

nosing, that part of the tread or horizontal surface of a step which projects over the vertical portion. It often has a small moulding beneath it.

Palladian window, a decorative grouping of three windows. It consists of a round-topped window flanked by two narrower, flat-topped ones, their height determined by the straight, vertical part of the middle one. In ornate examples this group may be surmounted by a small gable.

panel, a solid piece of wood framed in

between rails and stiles *q.v.*, as in a blind, door, or wainscot. It is usually flat. If its edges are beveled it is called a "raised panel." If it is of the same thickness as the members that frame it, it is a "flush panel."

parting strip, the strip of wood on the inside of a window frame that separates the two spaces in which the upper and lower sash slide up and down.

pedestal, a rectangular block, often with its own cap and base mouldings, which supports a column or pilaster.

pediment, a decorative structural feature consisting of cornice, frieze, and architrave, *qq.v.*, used in the Colonial gable or eaves.

piazza, also called veranda, or sometimes porch.

pier, a masonry column supporting timbers that carry heavy loads.

pilaster, a thin, *flat* column set against a wall.

plank, as used in this book, a board is an inch thick while a plank is two or more inches thick.

plate, the top member of the frame of a wall that carries the rafters and sometimes the attic floor beams.

porch, a small projection in front of an entrance. It may have a roof carried on posts, or may be closed in with its own walls. It differs from a veranda or piazza, which runs the full length of the house.

portico, a row of four or more columns, two stories high, set out from the front of the house, forming a large porch. Its pediment is usually part of the roof of the house.

quoin, a rectangular block of stone on the corners of masonry walls to tie them together. Sometimes copied in wooden buildings as a decorative feature, in place of the usual corner boards or similar treatments.

rafters, sloping roof-timbers carrying the roof covering and its load. Never properly called a roof beam.

rails, horizontal members separating panels, as in a door, and framing into the stiles, *q.v.* See *chair rail, handrail.*

reeding, a decoration consisting of small half-rounds side by side, something like corduroy. The opposite of fluting, *q.v.*

return, a short extension of a cornice or entablature carried around the corner to receive the gable mouldings.

riser, the vertical part of a step. See *tread.*

scale, an architectural word dealing with proportion. In a drawing, refers to dimensions of work as related to actual size. Example: $\frac{1}{4}$ inch equals one foot. In buildings relates to the dimensions of actual work to some unit of reference such as the height of a man or the size of a house. In the latter case exterior details should be larger than similar ones indoors if both are to be "in scale."

shutters, similar to blinds, *q.v.*, but with solid paneling in place of louvers.

sill, the horizontal bottom framing member that supports the wall of a house. It rests on the masonry foundation. Also, the bottom piece of a door or window opening which may be of stone or wood.

spindles, synonym for balusters, *q.v.* Used for very plain thin rectangular upright supports of the hand rail of a staircase.

stile, one of the vertical members of paneling as in a door, receiving the rails, *q.v.*

stop cut, a wood carver's term for the abrupt termination of a groove made by a gouge held in a vertical position.

string, the sloping support of stairs or steps of wood. If the ends of the steps do not show, it is a closed string; if they do, it is an open string, which is the usual form.

stud, a modern framing timber of manifold uses, often called "two by four" but actually at present nearly half an inch smaller in each dimension. Often doubled at door and window openings. A group of four, nailed together in L-shape, may be used in place of corner posts in the frame.

summer beam, in framed construction, a stout timber placed midway in height between the sill and the plate. It receives the ends of the floor beams and girders which are framed into it with mortise and tenon joints.

top out, to finish the top of a chimney in an appropriate manner.

tread, the flat or horizontal part of a step.

triglyph, in wooden architecture an upright board or series of boards in the frieze, extending from architrave to cornice. Often ornamented with V-shaped grooves (usually three) or flutes, rarely with reeds.

trunnel (tree nail), a wooden peg driven into a tightly fitting hole to secure two timbers connected by a mortise and tenon or similar joint.

wainscot, a covering for interior walls which may be the full height of the room or less, consisting of panels and the usual stiles and rails. If low, has a moulding as a cap.

wing, an appendage of a building, its axis parallel to the length of the house. See *ell*.

INDEX